GABON

WESTVIEW PROFILES • NATIONS OF CONTEMPORARY AFRICA
Larry W. Bowman, Series Editor

Gabon: Beyond the Colonial Legacy, James F. Barnes

*Guinea-Bissau: Power, Conflict, and Renewal
in a West African Nation,* Joshua B. Forrest

Namibia: The Nation After Independence,
Donald L. Sparks and December Green

Zimbabwe: The Terrain of Contradictory Development,
Christine Sylvester

*Mauritius: Democracy and Development in
the Indian Ocean,* Larry W. Bowman

Niger: Personal Rule and Survival in the Sahel, Robert B. Charlick

*Equatorial Guinea: Colonialism, State Terror, and the Search
for Stability,* Ibrahim K. Sundiata

Mali: A Search for Direction, Pascal James Imperato

Tanzania: An African Experiment,
Second Edition, Revised and Updated, Rodger Yeager

Cameroon: Dependence and Independence, Mark W. DeLancey

*São Tomé and Príncipe: From Plantation Colony
to Microstate,* Tony Hodges and Malyn Newitt

Zambia: Between Two Worlds, Marcia M. Burdette

Ethiopia: Transition and Development in the Horn of Africa,
Mulatu Wubneh and Yohannis Abate

Mozambique: From Colonialism to Revolution, 1900–1982,
Allen Isaacman and Barbara Isaacman

GABON

Beyond the Colonial Legacy

James F. Barnes

Westview Press

BOULDER • SAN FRANCISCO • OXFORD

Westview Profiles/Nations of Contemporary Africa

Copyright © 1992 by Westview Press, Inc.

Published in 1992 in the United States of America by Westview Press, Inc., 5500 Central Avenue, Boulder, Colorado 80301-2847, and in the United Kingdom by Westview Press, 36 Lonsdale Road, Summertown, Oxford OX2 7EW

Library of Congress Cataloging-in-Publication Data
Barnes, James Franklin, 1934–
    Gabon : beyond the colonial legacy / James F. Barnes.
        p.   cm. — (Westview profiles. Nations of contemporary Africa)
    Includes bibliographical references and index.
    ISBN 0-8133-0430-X
    1. Gabon—History—1960–   . I. Title.   II. Series.
DT546.18.B37   1992
967.2104—dc20   91-46627
                                                                                              CIP

Printed and bound in the United States of America

The paper used in this publication meets the requirements
of the American National Standard for Permanence of Paper
for Printed Library Materials Z39.48-1984.

10   9   8   7   6   5   4   3   2   1

To David Barnes,
for his courage and companionship

Contents

List of Tables
and Illustrations

Acknowledgments

I first visited Gabon in spring 1981, coincidentally at the time of François Mitterrand's first presidential victory in France. Thanks to a Fulbright, I returned to Gabon in 1983 to teach at the Université Omar Bongo (UOB), the national university of Gabon. I had naively expected to be able to offer the courses in politics that I had described in detail in my Fulbright application. It was then that I received my introduction to the realities of Gabonese politics. My assignment to teach a seminar in literature was a decision, I soon realized, that was designed to preclude the subversion of Gabon's best and brightest. Despite my initial disappointment, the seminar I taught in comparative literature was one of the most memorable experiences of my stay in Gabon. My students responded well to my predicament, and my virtually makeshift plan to explore such diverse authors as Aimé Césaire and Aleksandr Solzhenitsyn provided a rare opportunity to explore the meaning of intellectual freedom and human rights in a political environment not particularly well known for its dedication to these principles.

Along the way, I amassed a considerable debt to a number of persons who played various roles in my education about Gabon and the preparation of this profile. The soul of the book is the result of hours of patient instruction in the ways of Gabonese life and politics by my colleagues and students at UOB, and I owe an eternal debt of gratitude to Idalina Alves and Pierre Bernard, with whom a postlecture discussion during my first visit to Gabon developed into a warm and enriching friendship. I should also thank the directorate and staff of the Gabon National Library and Archives who, most unbureaucratically, accommodated my many requests for assistance.

The manuscript reflects the contribution of several people at pivotal moments in its origin and evolution. I am most indebted to series editor Larry Bowman, whose critical comments and encouragement helped to improve an early draft in dramatic need of assistance; Mildred Lewis and

Winston Van Horne intervened at a critical moment during the writing; and I owe Heather Paige Preston a special note of appreciation for her editing and review of several versions of the manuscript.

Dolly French and Linda Chapman deserve medals for their secretarial skills and services, and I am personally and professionally grateful to the Ohio University Department of Political Science, the Cartography Center of the Ohio University Geography Department, and the Ohio University Research Committee for their assistance and support.

In addition to the contributions of this diverse collection of friends, colleagues, and students, Mary Henrietta Kingsley's account of her remarkable journey in *Travels in West Africa* provided the initial intellectual spark.

Each of the persons and institutions that I have acknowledged has contributed in some important way, but the responsibility for any errors is, obviously, mine.

James F. Barnes

Introduction

On August 17, 1960, the French colony of Gabon became an independent republic. At the time, Libreville, the capital city, had fewer than 30,000 residents, and Gabon's principal port city and "economic capital," Port Gentil, was slightly smaller. Unlike its former fellow colonies Senegal and the Ivory Coast, or its most immediate neighbors, Cameroon and the Congo Republic, Gabon was relatively unknown and was, in fact, overshadowed by these more prestigious countries. Although thirty years have now passed, and Libreville and Port Gentil are no longer sleepy colonial outposts, Gabon is hardly a common name in the global geopolitical vocabulary, and its economic status and conservative reputation appear to set it apart from the other countries of the region. Although Gabon is obviously a part of Africa and African history, it appears to deny its place in that world while at the same time experiencing the consequences of its African identity.

Located on the Atlantic coast, Gabon borders the Gulf of Guinea and is bounded on the north by Equatorial Guinea and the Cameroon Republic and on the south and east by the People's Republic of the Congo (see Figure I.1). With a landmass of 267,537 square kilometers, Gabon is approximately the same size as the U.S. state of Colorado and is larger than Ireland or Ghana and half the size of France. Population figures, however, are a matter of debate. According to the government of Gabon and the official publications of the United Nations and other international agencies, Gabon's population is between 1.1 and 1.3 million inhabitants; more skeptical observers suggest that the number 900,000 is probably more accurate. Gabon's last credible national census was in 1960, when the population was determined to be approximately 450,000. Given Gabon's chronically low birth rate and its relatively high rate of infant mortality, it is highly unlikely that the population has tripled in size in thirty years. The official population figures reflect the government's obvious awareness of the relationship between the size of a nation's popu-

1

2

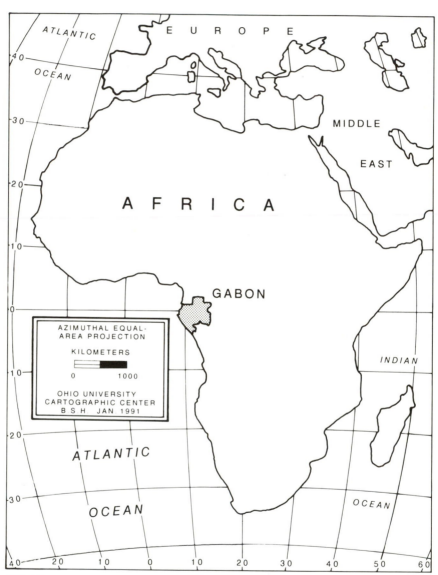

FIGURE I.1   Regional Setting of Gabon

lation and its eligibility for various forms of bilateral and multilateral economic assistance. However, one factor that may lend some credibility to the official figures is the steady increase in the number of non-Gabonese Africans working in the country; this figure could be as high as 200,000.

In striking contrast to its relatively small size, Gabon is a country of substantial mineral wealth. Major petroleum reserves are located in several areas along the Atlantic coast, and the northeastern and southeastern regions are sites of major deposits of iron ore, manganese, and uranium.

Gabon's topography is as varied as its abundant natural resources. The landscape ranges from savanna lands and dense tropical forests, which make up 85 percent of the territory, to the Cristal Mountains in the north, the du Chaillu massif in the center of the country, and the plateaus of the Haut Ogooué in the southeast near Gabon's border with the Congo Republic. Topographically, forests are Gabon's most prominent feature, and until the commercialization of its petroleum reserves in the mid-twentieth century, wood products were the primary source of national revenue. The isolation of Gabon's forests has effectively limited timber production and provided a degree of protection against the destruction that has occurred in many of the world's great tropical forests. Although Gabon's economy is significantly less dependent on its forests than it has been in the past, Gabon's rain forests are endangered, as are the rain forests of Brazil and other countries.

Gabon's location astride the equator adds a distinctive tropical character to its climate. The country's weather pattern includes relatively high humidity and substantial rainfall in most areas. In Libreville, rainfall averages 3,000 mm (117 inches) per year, and the average temperature is 25.9°C (78.6°F). The tropical heat is tempered by the cooling effect of the Benguéla current, which moves northward along the Gabon coast, creating a virtually permanent breeze in the immediate coastal areas. Throughout the country, temperatures range from 21°C (70°F) to 28°C (82°F).

Although there are minor variations in climate and rainfall throughout the country, there are, generally, two rainy and two dry seasons in Gabon: The long rainy season is from September through mid-December, followed by a short dry season that lasts until mid-February. The short rainy season then begins, lasting until mid-May and the beginning of the long dry season. In September, the cycle begins again with torrential rainfall in many areas of the country. The average rainfall in Libreville in October, the middle of the long rainy season, is 521.9 mm (20.35 inches). During periods of intense rainfall, transportation is disrupted, particularly in the logging areas, and the distribution of fruits and vegetables from the agricultural regions and neighboring Cameroon and the Congo Republic is severely curtailed. There is a substantial variation in seasonal temperatures and rainfall from the north to the south and from the coastal areas toward the interior. Areas in the coastal region, such as Cocobeach near the border with Equatorial Guinea, receive substantially more rainfall than areas such as Booué in the mid-interior, and the average temperature in Bitam, in the northernmost province of the Woleu N'Tem, is five degrees cooler than Libreville or Port Gentil. The highest recorded temperature in the country was 37.2°C (98.9°F) at Mouila in the southwest in 1951, and the lowest temperature on record is 10°C (50°F) at Mekambo in the northeast in 1964.

Gabon's major river, the Ogooué, in conjunction with its primary tributaries, the Ivindo and Okano in the north and the N'Gounié, the Lolo and the Offoué in the south, creates an extensive irrigation and transportation system that serves virtually the entire national territory. The Ogooué drains into the Atlantic at Port Gentil, completely traversing the country from its headwaters in the Congo Republic.[1]

Gabon's physical attributes explain the country's uniqueness and provide the key to understanding its evolution as an entity in the framework of European colonization and African history from the fifteenth century to the present. Initially, the maritime instincts of European visitors led them to explore the possibilities of the Gabon estuary, followed by efforts to commercialize the region's natural and physical resources—ivory and slaves, wild rubber, wood from the *okoumé* tree, and, in the twentieth century, petroleum, manganese, and uranium.

At the beginning of the 1990s, the people of Gabon find themselves at a critical juncture. President El Hadj Omar Bongo's announcement on May 21, 1990, of the end of one-party rule and the launching of a potentially new era of democracy represents the most significant challenge to the people of Gabon since their independence from France in 1960. It is a challenge that comes at a time of great prosperity and growing tension. Although many countries, including France and the United States, rationalized Bongo's authoritarian rule as a necessary condition for economic growth and stability, others considered Gabon's one-party state as a simple denial of the universal right of persons to choose their own destinies. For many years it was only possible for the Gabonese to praise Caesar; the possibility may now exist for the Gabonese to take a definitive step in the direction of self-government. The outcome of this process will involve the Gabonese themselves, the French, whose various interests in Gabon persist, and an array of other actors and observers, some of whom will judge the outcome as an indication of the future of the continent itself. As the people of Gabon take their future into their own hands, perhaps for the first time, it is my hope that readers of this book will gain an understanding of the country's arrival at this critical point.

NOTES

1. Information on geography, population, topography, climate, and natural resources compiled from Ministère de l'éducation nationale de la république gabonaise, *Géographie et cartographie du Gabon* (Paris: Editions classique d'expression française, 1981), pp. 22–24.

1

Early History to Independence

Gabon's identity as a modern nation-state is marked indelibly by its long-standing relationship with Europe and the United States. Prospects of substantial wealth have brought a host of Western explorers, slavers, soldiers, and missionaries to its shores since the initial contact in the mid-fifteenth century, during the celebrated era of European exploration. Within this broad historical context, Gabon emerged as a socioeconomic and, later, political entity reflecting the impact of outsiders on its evolution. Gabon's vast mineral wealth was the source of foreign interest in its affairs, and the international competition for control of its wealth provided the framework for its development over the past four centuries. Gabon's wealth remains its primary national asset and the key to an understanding of its emergence within the context of European colonial expansion.

PRECOLONIAL GABON

Very little is known today about those who inhabited the country before the fifteenth century. The people usually acknowledged to be the first Gabonese are the Babongo, the forest people or Pygmies, whose movement throughout central Africa appears to have preceded the arrival of the more powerful and numerous Bantu. The vast majority of Gabon's current population are the progeny of complex Bantu groups that spread throughout central and southern Africa. Adverse climatic conditions, the decline and fall of traditional central African kingdoms, and Islamic incursions across the Sahara are cited as the most likely reasons for the Bantu displacement from their ancestral lands. Scholars have proposed a number of hypotheses to explain the geographical locus of the origin of Bantu civilization and the pattern of its dispersion throughout sub-Saharan Africa. The most widely held view is that the Bantu came from the Lake Chad region at the southern edge of the Sahara. According to this view, either in search of new lands or fleeing hostile Arabs, the Bantu dispersed and migrated toward the south, eventually settling in the vast, diversified regions that comprise such modern states as Angola, the Central African Republic, the Congo Republic, Gabon, Swaziland, Zaire, and Zimbabwe. This thesis is subscribed to by the Gabonese historian Frédéric Meyo-Bibang, who poses the legendary Peul of the Lake Chad region as the ancestors of the Gabonese. In Meyo-Bibang's formulation, the Peul moved initially toward the south-central interior regions, then, at an indeterminate time, branched out toward the coastal and far southern areas of the continent. In his estimation, the first Bantu arrived in Gabon in the eleventh century.[1]

Meyo-Bibang's view is shared by the Senegalese scholar Cheikh Anta Diop, whose work supports the thesis of Saharan origin of the Bantu peoples.[2] A more recent and conflicting view suggests the modern-day province of Shaba in Zaire as the Bantu homeland, with successive migrations, accompanied by ethnolinguistic evolution, occurring in an enlarging series of irregular concentric circles.[3] This dispute about origins touches on an important issue: Are any African civilizations indigenous, or do they derive from the ancient civilizations of the Fertile Crescent, spreading into North Africa and southward, millennia ago? The question is both historical and ideological—for Africans and Europeans—in that issues of identity, pride, and historical certainty are intertwined. Although the archaeological work to date points to the African origins of *Homo sapiens*, a significant body of European scholarship has consistently portrayed Africa and the Africans as relatively insignificant participants in the origins and evolution of civilization. The corresponding idea that Africans are intellectually and spiritually inferior to persons of European origin continues to provide an important justification for outside efforts to control the affairs of the continent.

Substantial gaps remain in the history of the Bantu and Gabon's current population, and ongoing archaeological work has only recently provided even a tentative outline of a Gabonese prehistory. Several recent discoveries substantiate the presence of established communities in the coastal regions in the seventh century A.D., and a major discovery at Ikengué in the maritime Ogooué province in 1986 provides fragmentary evidence of a communal presence in 1300 B.C. The Ikengué finds cast considerable doubt on the conventional wisdom that the first Gabonese arrived only shortly before the Europeans. Clearly, much remains to be done, but archaeological investigations are limited by both Gabon's dense forest cover and a lack of funds. Only in the 1980s have professional archaeologists undertaken systematic research beyond the region of the estuary.[4]

Certainly by the fifteenth century, three major Bantu groups inhabited coastal Gabon: the Mpongwé in the northern region, the Orungu in
the Cap Lopez area, and the Nkomi in the Fernan Vaz. It is not certain,
however, how long these groups had resided in their respective areas or
what their relationship is to others of Bantu origin to the north and south
of Gabon. Historians generally agree that these groups were the heirs of
a powerful, somewhat mysterious, kingdom that may have dominated the
entire northern coast. Ruled by the legendary Mani-Pongo, this centralized
kingdom was in all probability, according to Elikia M'Bokolo, dominated
by the Ndiwa clan, reputed to be the first of the Mpongwé clans to reach
the coast and the first to encounter the Europeans in the fifteenth century.[5]
In his study of the northern Gabon coast, Karl David Patterson considered
whether Gabon was an isolated backwater or an area where the great
cultures of Nigeria-Cameroon and the southern Loanga kingdom over-
lapped.[6] Patrilineal traditions among the Mpongwé (as well as among the
Fang, who arrived in the nineteenth century) and matrilineal traditions
among the Orungu suggest strong influences of the patrilineal Nigeria-
Cameroon kingdom and the matrilineal Loanga kingdom on the shape of
the emerging Gabonese culture.[7]

The prominent Gabonese historian, André Raponda-Walker, subscribed to the view that the Mpongwé migrated to the northern coast in
the tenth century. After examining the records of French missionaries and
the oral history of the Mpongwé, he concluded that they originated in the
upper Ivindo region. (In sharp contrast to the conventional wisdom of
historians, legends of the Ndiwa clan of the Mpongwé hold that their
ancestors sprang spontaneously from the ground of the estuary region.) It
seems that the Mpongwé did migrate from the interior, but the dates of
their arrival in Gabon and subsequent movement toward the northern
coastal region remain unsubstantiated.

In Raponda-Walker's view, the Orungu—distinguishable from the
Mpongwé by their decidedly different inheritance traditions—came from
the south, adopting the language and customs of the coastal regions.[8] The
Gabonese historian Joseph Ambouroue-Avaro, in a distinctly different
view, suggested that the two peoples share a single ethnolinguistic heritage. He proposed that the Mpongwé and Orungu evolved from a matrilineal core zone including the south-central N'Gounié region and the
middle Ogooué area in central Gabon. The differences in inheritance
traditions, Ambouroue-Avaro argued, could reflect exposure to the different kingdoms to the north and south rather than a difference in origins.
Significantly, the two groups share a common language, and both are
included in a broad ethnolinguistic grouping using the expression *myéné*
(I say that) to initiate conversation.

For the novice, the linguistic and ethnic distinctions at work in Gabon are often challenging. While Myéné, for example, refers to a linguistic relationship, Omyéné is a collective noun that connotes a common ethnicity in addition to the linguistic meaning. A similar confusion exists in the distinction between Téké and Batéké, or Kota and Bakota. Téké and Kota are used to define linguistic parameters, while Batéké and Bakota refer to a broader ethnic identity. To advance the confusion, in everyday speech, individuals might be referred to as one or the other; as in "he is a Téké," or "she is a member of the Batéké group"; and it should be noted that although one might learn to speak Kota, one does not necessarily become a member of the Bakota group.

The "Omyéné cluster," including the Adjumba, Enenga, and Galoa, may, as Ambouroue-Avaro proposed, represent a common lineage. It is equally plausible, however, that a process of absorption and acculturation occurred in which unrelated groups were subordinated to others, and some speculate that the Orungu may have been a branch of the non-Myéné-speaking Eshira, who learned the art of navigation and the Myéné language from their extensive contacts with the neighboring Adjumba. Ambouroue-Avaro shared the burden placed on many scholars of Bantu history: Beyond the obvious quest for historical certainty, the issue of origins is a critical one in establishing the national identity of the contemporary Gabonese. It has long been held by Europeans that Gabon was simply an artifact of European civilization. Ambouroue-Avaro dedicated himself to formulating a history of Gabon that demonstrated the existence of a coherent, indigenous precolonial culture that could serve as the basis for a uniquely Gabonese identity in the postindependence era. His work, curtailed by his death in a plane crash in 1978, illustrates through its inconclusiveness the inherent difficulty in providing a credible record that satisfies both historical and ideological tests.[9]

The other members of the Omyéné cluster, the Adjumba, the Galoa, and the Enenga, lived in the lake country of the central Ogooué region. The regions farther in the interior were inhabited by groups who arrived over many centuries. The Tshogo and the Pindji, cited by Ambouroue-Avaro as likely progenitors of the Mpongwé, occupied the south-central regions near the present-day towns of Mouila and Sindara. To the east and the south, uncoordinated migrations of peoples from the present-day Congo Republic and Zaire completed the mix of the Gabonese population of the fourteenth and fifteenth centuries.

It is extraordinarily difficult to assess the significance of Gabon's precolonial era for the makeup and character of its contemporary institutions; it is not evasive to say that this is a world still described by fragmentary and conflicting evidence. It seems that the most important influences are represented in the traditions of magic and sorcery as detailed by Raponda-Walker and Roger Sillans in their study of indigenous Gabonese rituals and beliefs.[10] These traditions of animism and ancestor worship reflect a general belief held by all the diverse Gabonese groups in a divine guidance, expressed through the intermediary of ancestors and those who possess the power to establish communication among the occupants of this special universe. The Gabonese propensity for male and female secret societies and the persistence of sorcerers in contemporary Gabon represent important perceptions of the universe. Raponda-Walker's conclusion that Gabon's spiritual traditions were compatible with the tenets of Christianity provided for a corresponding synthesis between indigenous and foreign worlds.

EUROPEAN EXPLORATION
AND EARLY COMMERCE

European contact with Gabon began in 1472 when Portuguese ships commanded by Lopo Gonçalvez entered the estuary formed by the broad mouth of the Como River as it drains into the Atlantic. The Portuguese likened the estuary to a hooded cloak, or *gabão*, giving a permanent name, as well, to the country that would emerge in the twentieth century. Gonçalvez's expedition was part of a concerted Portuguese effort designed by Prince Henry the Navigator and continued by his successor, Alphonse VI, to counter Arab domination of the Mediterranean and Red Sea trade routes. The Portuguese strategy soon led to the spectacular discoveries of Magellan and Columbus as other monarchs and adventurers entered the race for the exotic goods of the Orient. For three years, from bases on São Tomé and Príncipe and Rio Muni, expeditions led by Gonçalvez and Diego Cão explored and charted the coastal areas, preparing the way for further expeditions and permanent settlements.

The arrival of Europeans fundamentally altered the nature of life in the coastal areas. The introduction of European commerce generated conflict among the indigenous residents and engendered a transformation of their political, economic, and social institutions. Elikia M'Bokolo, who has written extensively on Gabon, described this period as characterized by three *unités microrégionales*, that is, concentrations of Mpongwé, Orungu, and Nkomi in their respective geographical areas.

Until the advent of commercial exchanges with the Europeans, the northern coast appears to have been characterized by substantial harmony and interchange between the major Mpongwé clans. Their principal economic activities included subsistence farming, hunting, and fishing; each settlement maintained artisans who produced a range of utensils and items required for religious ceremonies. Patterson noted the copper bracelets worn by Mpongwé women at this time as evidence of possible trade with the southern Loanga kingdom. Certainly, the Mpongwé were skilled sailors; there are numerous reports of Mpongwé expeditions along the coast in large dugout canoes, venturing as far north as the Cameroon River.

The microregional equilibrium was shattered by aggressive Orungu efforts to usurp the Mpongwé's commercial advantage. Control of the prized role as intermediary to the Europeans stimulated competition between these two major groups and with others in the interior who increasingly abandoned traditional economic practices to participate in the commerce of the coast. The Orungu, moving northward from their base in the Ogooué delta, overwhelmed several peripheral Mpongwé clans, including the Adjumba, before mounting a direct attack on the major Mpongwé clans, notably the Ndiwa and Benga, effectively limiting these clans to the region of the estuary. According to M'Bokolo, the Orungu benefited from a strong, centralized governing system that had not, as yet, undergone the fragmentation experienced by the Mpongwé.[11] The gradual disintegration of these centralized political systems was brought about by destabilizing influences introduced by European commerce and trade.

The region of the estuary formed by the Como River as it enters the Atlantic Ocean became the critical battleground for these competing groups. The banks of the estuary became havens for the Mpongwé clans that sought protection from the incursions of the Orungu. By the beginning of the nineteenth century, the three major groups, Mpongwé, Orungu, and Nkomi, appear to have reached a momentary stability. Restricted by Orungu strategy from access to the region of the estuary, the Nkomi consolidated their control of the Fernan Vaz, entering actively in the trade and commerce of the lower Ogooué delta.

The historical record indicates active Portuguese commerce along the Gabonese coast throughout the sixteenth century, and Gabon's geopolitical vocabulary bears its imprint; such names as Sette Cama, Fernan Vaz, and Cap Lopez attest to the Portuguese presence. Portuguese ships carried away cargoes of ivory and palm oil, and by the early 1700s, slaves for the American markets. The Dutch were also attracted by the prospects of commerce with the indigenous population. Throughout the sixteenth and seventeenth centuries, Dutch ships visited the Gabon coast regularly, returning to Europe with an array of goods. Increasingly, Dutch and Portuguese sailors and merchants were joined by ships displaying the colors of other European countries. By the end of the seventeenth century, Cap Lopez, charted by the Portuguese in the late 1400s, had become a regular port of call for European and American ships in search of ivory, palm oil, and such exotic goods as parrot feathers and the teeth of hippopotami, and both Protestant and Catholic missionaries arrived to convert the indigenous peoples to Christianity. Holland, Denmark, France,

Great Britain, and Germany attempted, at different times, to establish permanent settlements in Gabon, initially along the banks of the estuary and later at such strategic locations as Ndjolé and Lambaréné on the Ogooué River. Relations between the competitors were hardly amicable; the prospects for material and evangelical rewards produced discord and overt hostility among the Europeans and fostered enmity between the Gabonese residents of the estuary and the newcomers.[12]

As the New World colonies developed and the demand for slave labor intensified, ships from Europe and the Americas visited the west African coast regularly, and Gabon became a source of supply for the increasingly lucrative slave trade. Traffic in slaves from Gabon never reached the proportions of the trade on the Slave Coast to the north or along the Loanga coast, in the area to the south that is now Angola. Gabon's topography and relatively small population limited its attractiveness to slavers interested in large concentrations of young men and women who could be gathered easily near the coast. In the eighteenth century, Gabon's population probably did not exceed 150,000, with a substantial proportion of this number living in the inaccessible interior. In addition, of the two principal navigational routes used by slavers, the first or *petite* route, which took the slavers slowly along the coast of the Gulf of Guinea, was less favored than the *grande* route, which bypassed Gabon on a direct course to the more plentiful supply of slaves along the densely populated Loanga coast to the south. The *grande* route further gave the slave ships the full advantage of the trade winds on the journey to the markets of the New World.

The issue of African involvement in the slave traffic remains controversial. Considerable evidence supports the assertion that the Mpongwé and Orungu were active participants. Patterson described Dutch and Portuguese sales of slaves to the Mpongwé, among whom slavery appears to have been already established. In their complicated social stratification system, slaves were important in determining the owner's wealth and status; it was customary for slaves of important Mpongwé to be interred alive with their deceased owners. Persons could be enslaved for a variety of reasons, such as punishment for a crime, defeat in battle, or debt. Slavers from Europe and the Americas exploited this customary practice with their offers of exotic new goods, expanding—and distorting—it into a profitable economic venture. In these days, a healthy young slave went for a dozen pounds of salt, a rifle, and a barrel of gunpowder. As the trade expanded, Mpongwé brokers assisted by peoples of the interior like the Obamba and Adouma supplied slaves to auction sites near the coast. Although the trade in slaves in Gabon never attained major proportions, it was intense in the southern maritime regions, in part because Gabon's network of navigable rivers, particularly in the southeastern Ogooué basin, facilitated the supplying of slaves to the coast. The number of slaves exported from Gabon is estimated at several thousand per year during the peak period between 1815 and 1830. As these dates indicate, the traffic continued well after the formal abolition of the slave trade by the United States and the major European powers in 1815.[13]

By the 1700s, Portuguese interests had settled on the Loanga kingdom (Angola) and Brazil. Aside from São Tomé and Príncipe, the Portuguese failed to maintain a commercial presence in the Gulf of Guinea, leaving the competition principally to the Dutch, British, Germans, and North Americans. In the mid-1800s, U.S. interests initiated an important evangelical offensive under the sponsorship of the American Board of Commissioners for Foreign Missions (ABCFM); missionaries representing several major Protestant denominations soon established missions along the northern Gabonese coast.

Like the Portuguese, the Dutch actively engaged in commerce with Mpongwé residents of the estuary. The Mpongwé, notably the Ndiwa, were not, however, always hospitable hosts. In 1600, apparently to prevent direct Dutch trade with groups in the interior, the Ndiwa stormed the Dutch settlement on Corisco Island. It is commonly assumed that the Dutch massacre of the Ndiwa in 1698 was a belated response to this Ndiwa attack, but Patterson rejected this explanation, citing evidence that the Ndiwa had abandoned the region by the late 1600s—and suggesting the implausibility of the Dutch waiting nearly a hundred years for revenge. Whatever the historical circumstances, by the early 1700s, Ndiwa influence on the northern coast had clearly declined, and the era of the powerful Pongo kingdom was ending. According to Raponda-Walker, what remained of the kingdom in the eighteenth century was a collection of clans, each led by an *oga* (plural, *aga*), or chief. The Mpongwé clans of the estuary engaged in an annual ritual that elevated one of the chiefs to a position as first among equals.[14] The position of *oga* carried with it important religious duties, and the residence of the *oga* was the repository for important religious relics, which the *oga* was responsible for safeguarding against loss or capture by an enemy. The *oga* also became critically important as the need for an interlocutor between the clans and the Europeans and, later, Americans became necessary.

In the long line of *aga* representing the clans of the estuary and their collective interests, Antchouwé Kowe Rapontchombo, called King Dénis by the French and King William by the British and Americans, was the most significant indigenous figure in the emerging pattern of relationships between the residents of the estuary and the foreigners. Born in 1780, Rapontchombo served as *oga* of the Asiga clan from 1810 until his death in 1876. Although decorated by the French and the British for assisting their commercial and religious ventures, he also played a decisive role in

The *oga* Antchouwé Kowe Rapontchombo with his senior wife, circa 1850 (photo courtesy of the Gabon National Archives).

limiting the early expansionist activities of the French, British, and Americans. In assessing his role in this critical formative period, M'Bokolo praised Rapontchombo as an early promoter of economic development, attempting to protect and conserve the essential qualities of indigenous life, although cautiously accepting the foreign presence. In contrast to his guarded acceptance of the French and British, Rapontchombo appears to have strenuously opposed the evangelical practices of Americans in the estuary. With forty wives and an apparent affinity for the good life, Rapontchombo personally contradicted the U.S. missionaries' puritanical view of polygamy and alcohol as grievous affronts to Christianity.[15]

In the early eighteenth century, the Dutch expanded their commercial contacts with the coast, increasingly including slaves in their cargoes. The Dutch were thus in direct competition with the Portuguese, who from their base on São Tomé and Príncipe were exporting significant numbers of slaves from the Loanga coast. The competition between the Dutch and the Portuguese continued until antislaver squadrons of the British and French navies effectively excluded them from the traffic in the mid-nineteenth century.

The arrival of the French in the Gulf represented a step in France's long-standing rivalry with Great Britain over naval rights along the African coast and in the Indian Ocean. Additionally, in 1815, France signed the Treaty of Vienna, agreeing, at least in principle, to a universal prohibition of the slave trade. Thus, the French came to the Gulf of Guinea to interdict the slave traffic as well as to continue their maritime rivalry with Great Britain over the control of strategically located naval stations. Clearly, the French also envied the commerical presence of the British in the estuary. Until the nineteenth century, French economic ventures in Africa were limited to Senegal, well to the north, but the French were not newcomers to the Gulf of Guinea—French ships may have visited Gabon as early as 1515.

EARLY FRENCH INITIATIVES

The establishment of a French presence in Gabon was the result of a convergence of naval and commercial interests. Initially sent to the region to carry out the French government's pledge to interdict the slave trade, the Dakar-based fleet soon acquired an important commerical role. Ships from the antislaver squadron ranged the west African coast from Dakar to the Loanga kingdom, following routes also used by French commerical ships. Increasingly, the navy was called upon to protect the personnel and cargoes of these ships from attacks by the coastal populations. As M'Bokolo pointed out, it was, quite ironically, Gabonese involvement in the traffic of slaves that brought about the initial instances of tension and conflict between the indigenous populations of the coast and the crews of the antislaver squadrons.[16] For some time, the coastal Gabonese had been involved in the slave traffic and resisted efforts on the part of the French to limit their involvement. It appears that French commercial ships were regularly ransacked and pillaged, leading to a decision by French commercial interests in Dakar to call upon the navy for protection. The navy responded by expanding its protective role as well as intensifying its search for new bases for supply and maintenance of its ships. These various motives converged in the historic voyage of the frigate *Malouine* in 1837.

Commanded by the ambitious young officer Edouard Bouët-Willaumez, the *Malouine* sailed from Dakar in search of a suitable port for ships of the Atlantic fleet and, under orders from the naval commandant at Dakar, Montagniès de la Rocque, to assist in the search for new commercial sites as well as provide protection for French commercial interests in the region. Headquarters of the French fleet in Africa, Dakar was also the site of a growing French commercial presence in west Africa. Under pressure from navy and commercial interests in Le Havre and a consortium of investors in Nantes and Bordeaux, the French government initiated its policy of establishing fortified commercial-military sites, *points d'appui*, at strategic locations along the coast. The policy was supported energetically by Bouët and an influential colleague, Victor Calvé, who in addition to his position as a naval surgeon was a representative of the Nantes-Bordeaux group. The explicit mission of the *Malouine* reflected this complex coalescence of interests; Bouët's orders were to establish commercial sites, protect French commercial shipping, and intercept ships of any nation— including France—engaged in the slave trade.

Bouët arrived in the estuary of Gabon in 1839, on the first of a series of voyages that marked the beginning of a fateful French involvement with the Gabonese. The culmination of these initial visits was a series of treaties with the leading *aga* of the left and right banks of the estuary. The first of these treaties was with Rapontchombo and the Asiga clan on the left bank of the estuary. Three years later, in 1842, Bouët engaged France in a treaty with the *oga* of the right bank, Dowé, called King Louis by the French. In subsequent treaties with the *aga* of the remaining estuary lands, Bouët extended French control over a significant portion of northern coastal Gabon; and in the definitive treaty of August 1, 1846, France claimed "all the land that seemed appropriate for the creation of military and agricultural establishments." A concluding passage of the treaty ceded land to the French priest Jean Remy Bessieux for his missionary activities. In exchange, the *oga* Re'dembino, known to the French as King François, and the members of his Adoni clan became entitled to "whatever the government of France judged to be an appropriate annual contribution."[17]

Bouët's separate treaties with the various rulers of the estuary lands illustrate the significant changes in the disposition of power and authority that had taken place in the estuary. By the mid-nineteenth century, no single structure of authority remained to unite the various Myéné-speaking clans. The Dutch massacre of the Ndiwa and the incursion of the Orungu from the south had eroded the Mpongwé's predominant role, and the once powerful Pongo kingdom was reduced to a collection of clans. To the south, in the area that is now the Congo Republic and Angola, the Loanga kingdom exerted its claim over thousands of subjects, but its scope did not include the regions claimed by Bouët for France.

In the estuary, Bouët encountered the remnants of the northern kingdom in the clans governed by *aga* (the French called them kings), who exercised their authority only within limited kinship groups. The French established their dominance by creating a network of indigenous *aga* willing to express their loyalty to France. This was, for a time, a game with more than one player. The British and Germans also recruited patrons among the *aga*, and the region was, for many years, the scene of extensive competition among the Europeans and Americans for the favor of the indigenous authorities. In 1843, R'ogourowe, *oga* of the Agekaze clan, switched his allegiance from the British to the French at the instigation of

French officers who convinced him of a British plot to undermine his authority. For a number of years, plots involving a complicated cast of characters highlighted life in the region of the estuary. It was during the decade of the 1840s that the village of Glass, named apparently for the drinking habits of R'ogourowe (King Glass), became the center of the anglophone community of British and Americans and an important base for the French in their effort to eliminate their competitors from the estuary.[18]

At approximately the same time as the arrival of the *Malouine*, another event took place that was to have long-term consequences for the French and the Gabonese. British and American missionaries exploring the northern and central regions of the territory provided firsthand accounts of the appearance of Fang clans arriving from the north. The earliest recorded account had been made in 1819 by the British missionary Thomas Bowdich, who encountered the Fang, or Pahouins, as they were referred to at this time, in the northern-most regions of the territory—the area of present-day Equatorial Guinea and southern Cameroon. The Fang migration represented the final piece in a complicated ethnic puzzle that began with the Mpongwé movement from the interior to the coast. For the Fang, their encounter with the French was particularly noteworthy in that Fang legend had long prophesied the arrival of white warriors from the sea. To the French, the Fang were the answer to their prayers for energetic partners in their economic enterprises; the French idealized the newcomers as noble savages in contrast to the Mpongwé, who had been spoiled by their involvement with civilization. The arrival of the Fang in Gabon and their subsequent establishment as the single largest ethnic group in the country permanently altered the ethnic balance of power; the once-predominant Mpongwé suffered a lasting decline in their traditional hegemony in the estuary region.

In the ten years following Bouët's arrival, economic activity in the estuary noticeably increased. Two major French firms, Lecour of Nantes and Dubarry Frères of Le Havre; the British firms Hatton and Cookson, and John Holt; and the German firm Woermann competed for the ivory and wild rubber in the interior. The results of this intense competition were mixed and for the French, initially disappointing, as several promising ventures failed. Unaccustomed to life in the tropics, the new arrivals faced epidemics of malaria and yellow fever. Plantings of cotton and sugar cane, following the Portuguese precedent on São Tomé, often failed. Despite the apparent ease with which plants flourished in the tropics, mass production proved difficult; torrential rains ruined newly planted fields, and an unexpected shortage of manual labor emerged as an obstacle. Since the arrival of the Portuguese, the coastal Myéné-speaking groups had established themselves in the profitable business of intermediaries.

As brokers between the Europeans on the coast and the peoples of the interior, the Myéné traded slaves and ivory, successfully resisting European efforts to employ them as common field hands. Initially, the Europeans were content to remain aboard their ships, relying upon agents drawn from the coastal population to broker their exchanges with the interior, but dissatisfaction with the Mpongwé led the French to establish more direct trading practices. In addition to their growing reputation as dishonest brokers, the Mpongwé often failed to honor their agreements to provide labor for the plantations. It was, in fact, a novel attempt to resolve the labor crisis that led to the establishment of the settlement of Libreville. In the affair of the *Eliza*, the French found the answer to their labor dilemma.

The *Eliza*, a Dutch slaver seized by French ships in the Gulf of Guinea, carried 261 slaves bought at auctions along the Loanga coast. After the arrival of the ships in Dakar, French officials revived an earlier plan to transport the slaves to Gabon to work on the plantations. This plan violated the policy of the Ministry of the Navy, which exercised administrative control in the territories claimed by France during this era. Ministry rules explicitly prohibited slave labor in any territory under French jurisdiction. This obstacle was removed by a decision of the naval commandant at Dakar, Montagniès de la Rocque, that the slaves were automatically freed upon arriving in an area of French jurisdiction (an interesting episode in light of the Dred Scott controversy in the United States a decade later). De la Rocque envisaged two options for the newly freed slaves: return to Loanga and possible recapture by slavers or—de la Rocque's preference—work as wage laborers on the Gabonese plantations. There were, however, other obstacles. One hundred of the Loangans died from illness contracted during their passage, and many of the young women among the survivors were taken under the care and supervision of a religious order that refused to allow their participation in the venture.

The situation was salvaged with the replacement of de la Rocque as naval commandant by Bouët-Willaumez following changes in the goverment in Paris brought on by the revolutionary events of 1848. Pursuant to guidelines introduced originally by de la Rocque, Bouët recruited a small number of Loangans for the trip to Gabon. In order to safeguard the interests of the Loangans and to convince their protectors in Dakar of their future well-being, de la Rocque had provided for such matters as their religious instruction and their personal safety. In fact, as M'Bokolo observed, de la Rocque viewed the Loangans as the nucleus of a small community that would bear the important and timely responsibility of enhancing the French presence.[19] On August 8, 1849, Bouët arrived in Gabon with fifty-two survivors of the *Eliza* to found the village of Libreville near the site of Fort d'Aumale, the initial French encampment.

Events in the newly established "Freetown" did not proceed as Bouët and his associates planned. The Loangans were no more enthused about fieldwork than the Myéné. During their stay in Senegal, many of the former slaves had learned trades, and they resisted French efforts to force them to work on the plantations. Conflict arose between the Loangans and French religious leaders, notably Bessieux, who determined that morality dictated Christian marriage for the Loangans. At Bessieux's demand, partners were assigned by the French authorities, and a mass wedding took place, clearly against the wishes of many of the participants. Although the settlement survived, its early years were tentative and precarious.

For the Gabonese residents of the estuary, these years represented a critical juncture. One significant consequence of the foreign presence was the institution of a governing system that eroded the authority of the indigenous clan leaders. Despite the efforts of such key figures as Rapontchombo and Dowé to maintain their traditional bases of authority, European commercialization of trade led to a diminished role for these notables in the affairs of their people. For the Gabonese, status was increasingly measured in European terms, that is, in money or commodities used in commercial transactions. The traditional practice of bartering gave way to a cash nexus that altered, perhaps irreversibly, traditional methods of assessing and determining value. New occupations associated with the increase in trade and commerce led to a reorientation of relationships within the indigenous populations. Persons conscripted to serve as porters for expeditions into the interior and laborers on the plantations came increasingly into the orbit of control and authority imposed by the outsiders. Similarly, missionaries undermined the traditional structure of authority in their role as representatives and interpreters of a new cosmology. Aggressive Catholic and Protestant missionaries converted thousands to Christianity, imposing a new orthodoxy that supplemented and reinforced the power of the outsiders.

This process of change, initially uneven and sporadic, accelerated noticeably with the decision of the French to embark upon a more systematic attempt to enhance their position as an African power. The French had not initially shown interest in expanding their influence toward the interior regions. In 1844, in a message to the British, Foreign Minister François Pierre Guillaume Guizot stated that France would exercise an external sovereignty over the lands claimed by Bouët in treaties that had not, in fact, been ratified by the French National Assembly. French policy was premised on a determination to avoid conflict with Great Britain, with an accompanying mandate to support the fledgling colonies with the least possible expenditure of funds. The British, in turn, appeared reticent to provoke a war with the French over such a relatively minor economic

Bird's-eye view of the Gabon trading post from a sketch by the frigate captain H. Vallon (photo courtesy of the Gabon National Archives).

investment as Gabon. In a broader context both British and French policies reflected changes in the larger world of European politics. According to Bernard Schnapper in his study of French politics and commerce in the Gulf of Guinea, by the early 1840s both Britain and France had entered into a period of free trade that translated into a mutual tolerance for economic competition on Gabonese territory. The French were much less tolerant of British—or German—competition in their principal areas of interest, that is, Senegal and the region of the Ivory Coast. From the perspective of Paris, Gabon was initially a minor investment, whose significance in the colonial scheme of things developed later.[20]

Ten years elapsed between France's troubling defeat in its war with Germany in 1871 and the French capture of Tunis in 1881. During this period, a remarkable transformation occurred in French attitudes about colonial adventures, producing a complete revision of the government's policy toward tropical Africa. It was during this critical decade that the French became swept up in the general burst of European enthusiasm for projects and enterprises in faraway places. This was the era of Ferdinand de Lesseps and the Suez Canal, and the construction of great rail systems like the Union Pacific, designed to bring the Atlantic regions of the United States in touch with its new Pacific acquisitions. In France, before the defeat of 1871, there appears to have been no substantial interest in sub-Saharan Africa. The French were preoccupied with their conquests in Algeria and Indochina and, beyond Senegal, appeared content to leave other regions of the continent unattended.[21]

THE COLONIAL ERA

The discovery of gold and diamonds in southern Africa sparked a wave of explorations throughout black Africa. France, now intent on expanding its empire and repairing the damage done to both national pride and the national treasury by the loss of Alsace and Lorraine to the Germans, launched an ambitious effort to expand its holdings in equatorial Africa. During the period of Bouët's activities, the role of the French government in Gabon was, essentially, symbolic; after 1881, France increased its administrative, military, and financial commitment to equatorial Africa, elevating the status of the region and settling in for an extended stay. If any single event can be cited to illustrate the newly found enthusiasm of the French, it was the overwhelming interest of the government and public in the African expeditions of the young naval officer, Pierre Savorgnan de Brazza.

De Brazza, an Italian nobleman who became a naturalized French citizen, entered the French navy with an officer's commission in 1870. After serving in the Franco-German war, he visited Gabon and launched a new career as an explorer. It was commonly believed at the time that navigable waterways existed between the coast and the distant interior regions of the continent. After several unsuccessful attempts, three highly publicized voyages between 1874 and 1882 enabled de Brazza to demonstrate the accessibility of the Congo basin from the Gabon coast and in so doing, rival the achievements of Henry Morton Stanley and David Livingstone in the eyes of the French public. Although his discoveries made him a national hero, the more important result was the determination of the French government to press on with plans to establish a colonial system in tropical Africa. The imperialist scramble was on, and France joined with its European neighbors in a bid for the wealth of the continent.

By the mid-1880s, the interior of Gabon was thoroughly explored. Even before de Brazza's publicized efforts to discover a route to the Congo basin, the French-American adventurer Paul du Chaillu made a number of trips into the interior, during which he chronicled the Fang passage from the north. The interior regions were known also to French and U.S. missionaries; two U.S. missionaries, Ira Preston and William Walker, were the first foreigners to explore areas of the Ogooué basin near the present-day town of Lambaréné.

Gabon estuary, circa 1895 (photo courtesy of the Gabon National Archives).

On the basis of the observations of du Chaillu and de Brazza and other French explorers, most notably Alfred Marche and Louis Victor du Pont, the Marquis de Compiègne, the French government initiated a major effort to secure control of the territory now referred to as the Middle Congo. Agents from various commercial firms and a cadre of colonial administrators followed the routes of de Brazza and du Chaillu. Until 1881, administrative responsibility for the colonies had been exercised by the Ministry of the Navy, whose policies were determined by the naval strategies of the various maritime powers with interests along the west African coast. In 1881, the National Assembly shifted the responsibility for the colonies to the Ministry of Trade and Colonies and then, in 1894, to the new cabinet-level Ministry of the Colonies; these administrative changes illustrate the evolution of French colonial policy during this period.

Throughout the fifty-five years between Bouët's initial treaty with Rapontchombo in 1839 and the establishment of the Ministry of the Colonies in 1894, the situation in Gabon remained unsettled. Despite

French efforts, returns on investments were often disappointing, and the aggressive economic and evangelical activities of the British, Germans, and Americans raised alarm. Economic competition from the British and Germans was particularly worrisome. Although France claimed the lion's share of the land through its extensive treaties, the British retained a successful commercial presence, particularly in Libreville and several interior locations. From the north, through Cameroon, the Germans joined in the competition for wild rubber, ivory, and, somewhat later, the wood of the *okoumé* tree. In the contest for economic supremacy, the French were at a decided disadvantage. In a letter to his superior in 1883, the naval commandant of Gabon, Masson, complained of the lack of support from Paris and warned that the French were losing the trade battle to Woermann and Hatton and Cookson.[22]

To retain the loyalty of the *aga*, the French adopted a "policy of gifts," with regular deliveries to the indigenous notables. A second technique involved "son-in-law diplomacy"—the practice by some French commercial representatives of living in concubinage with the daughters of influential families. With regard to the gift policy, according to the contemporary Gabonese historian Ange Ratanga-Atoz, French merchandise was often inferior to that of the British and Germans, who were adept at the same practices. It seems that the French were often obliged to buy gifts from their competitors in order to maintain the allegiance of their patrons. Both the British and Germans maintained regular steamship routes from England and Germany to Gabon, and the absence of such a link to France furthered the French dependence on their competitors. The practice of concubinage provoked occasional outbursts of hostility among local families, but otherwise provided a relatively pleasant way for French merchants to insure favor and protect their economic interests.

On the evangelical front, the French confronted an active corps of U.S. missionaries whose schools and missionary services rivaled their own. A U.S. church and school flourished in the Baraka section of Libreville, and Presbyterian and Congregationalist missionaries traveled into the interior and southward along the coast. By the mid-1800s, a total of thirty-five missionaries had been assigned to Gabon by the American Board of Commissioners for Foreign Missions.

French intentions became increasingly focused in the early 1880s as intergovernmental squabbles about jurisdiction were resolved and the French undertook their first truly concerted effort to establish their dominance in the region. The evangelical competition between U.S. and French missionaries was resolved in favor of the French with the decision by the local administration in 1883 that French would be the only language of instruction in the mission schools. U.S. missionaries finally acceded to the French and transferred their activities to the Société des missions évangélique de Paris (SME), a French Protestant missionary group. After this decision, many of the U.S. missionaries moved north into Cameroon or southward away from the primary areas of French influence. Through the work of the SME, and later the Evangelical Church of Gabon, a strong Protestant presence persists in several areas of the country.

The future of Gabon had been a subject of negotiation between France and Great Britain for some time, reflecting the French government's long-standing ambivalence about the French presence in Gabon. In 1866, France appeared ready to exchange Gabon and two west African territories, Assinie and Grand Bassam, to the British for rights to the Gambia. This arrangement would have given France hegemony over all of the Senegalese territory and rid it of an area of unproven profitability. Negotiations between the two countries ended in 1876, following protracted discussions in which terms and conditions changed several times. Resistance to the idea was strong in Gabon among religious leaders like Bessieux. By the 1870s, Bessieux's order, the Fathers of the Holy Ghost, had made a substantial commitment in Gabon, expanding missionary activities over a broad geographical area. The French commercial houses were equally opposed to abandoning their investments, despite their often precarious financial status. The Ministry of the Navy opposed the loss of Gabon as a base for the Atlantic fleet. In France, Prime Minister Jules Ferry, leader of the Colonial party, presided over a National Assembly that agreed in principle with the logic of expanding French influence throughout the region. The French were particularly sensitive to the Belgian presence in the neighboring Congo and German initiatives in Cameroon. In a decisive move reflecting a newly found determination to make the region profitable, the French government implemented the concessionary policy adopted in the Belgian Congo and championed in France by the economist Paul Leroy-Beaulieu and Eugene Etienne, under secretary of state for the colonies and the founder of the Colonial party in the assembly. French and British interests were reconciled by the partition agreements of the Congress of Berlin (1884–1885), and Gabon became part of France's broadly based empire in central and west Africa even as Ferry's government fell in 1885 in response to French setbacks in Indochina.[23]

The concessionary system adopted for Gabon was based on the principle of granting territorial monopolies to private commercial firms, giving them virtually exclusive authority within their respective zones. In the following decade, the French government issued franchises to forty firms in the territory of the Middle Congo. Of the twelve firms authorized to operate in Gabon, the Société commerciale, industrielle et agricole du Haut Ogooué (SHO) was the largest and most notorious. The SHO received a territorial concession of 104,000 square kilometers, virtually half the country. Like other concessionary companies of the era, the SHO was interested in wild rubber and ivory, commodities that the companies gathered aggressively, depleting the natural growth and decimating herds of elephants in the process. In the fifteen years of its operation, the SHO established no permanent infrastructure and created a climate of animosity that endures to this day. All the concessions ruled absolutely, with authority to call upon the military for assistance; large concessions like the SHO maintained private militias, used to quell labor unrest or other disturbances within their jurisdictions. The concessions were notorious for the low prices they paid to obtain products. In return for their monopolies, the concessions were required to pay the colonial administration a nominal deposit, 15 percent of annual profits, and contribute to the maintenance of customs posts and telegraph lines within their concessionary areas. In reality, the concessions went about their business free of external interference and with minimum investment of their own capital. In many cases, payments to local producers were made in kind or in company currencies redeemable only in company-owned trading posts— a common colonial practice.

In the course of their activities, the concessions produced a record of abuses that created a furor in Paris. Although the French public generally supported colonial activities, reports of brutality disturbed those who saw colonialism as a means of sharing the benefits of European civilization with the less fortunate Africans. Continuing reports of brutal treatment prompted the government in Paris to dispatch de Brazza himself in the early 1900s on a mission of investigation during which he substantiated a pattern of universal and persistent brutality. The concessions were completely insensitive to the welfare of their workers and had no apparent interest in any form of economic development in the territories under their control. At this time, the number of French officials in the entire Middle Congo barely reached one hundred—an insufficient presence to exert any measure of control over the virtually autonomous concessionary companies.

Disenchantment with the concessionary system was not limited to the readers of de Brazza's report. Many of the firms became disappointed as they failed to realize significant returns on their investments; of the forty companies franchised initially, only a dozen appear to have been more than marginally successful. De Brazza's report led to the abandonment of the concessionary approach and a return to open competition between firms. Many of the former concession companies remained in Gabon and continued their search for ivory and rubber throughout the country.[24] Some years later, de Brazza's report was dramatically underscored by one of France's most respected writers, André Gide, following his highly publicized voyage to the tropics. Gide's polemic against the colonial system led to additional official investigations exposing the continuing extraordinary inhumanity of the firms. Describing the *colons*, one report stated, "Most of their principles seem to melt away in the tropical heat . . . and the Africans naturally bear the consequences."[25]

The demise of the concessionary approach prompted the French to apply the administrative model they had successfully used in French West Africa. In 1910, the French established a new federation, *Afrique équatoriale française* (AEF), comprising Gabon, the French Congo, Ubangi-Shari (later the Central African Republic), and Chad. Although Libreville was the first capital, Brazzaville was eventually chosen as the AEF headquarters. The federation was administered by a governor-general assisted by lieutenant-governors in the three regional capitals, Libreville, Bangui, and Fort Lamy (Ndjamena). Although Paris hailed the creation of the federation as a significant progressive step, Gabon's interests were subordinated to those of the other members of the federation, and tensions remained between Brazzaville and Libreville well into the postindependence era.

From the concessionary era to the outbreak of World War I, the major exports of the Gabonese economy remained rubber and ivory. Exports began to decline, however, as the herds of elephants were decimated and the once-plentiful stands of wild rubber were depleted. The French successfully reorientated the export economy to wood from the *okoumé* tree, the mainstay of the Gabonese economy until replaced by petroleum in the 1960s. A less expensive substitute for mahogany, *okoumé* was first harvested and marketed successfully by the Germans. Germany's loss of its African possessions following World War I allowed the French to monopolize the *okoumé* trade and, after World War II, enter the profitable plywood industry.

THE CIVILIZING MISSION AND THE ORIGINS OF GABONESE NATIONALISM

Throughout the period of colonial rule, French relations with the Gabonese were based on the French notion of the *mission civilatrice* (civilizing mission), that is, the obligation of the French to instruct Africans (and other lesser peoples) in the ways of French and European civilization. It was the moral duty of the French to transform the colonies into microcosms of the metropolis, and a carefully crafted policy of assimilation that would turn the indigenous peoples into copies of their new masters was perceived as the highest service that the French could provide to their subjects. In 1910, with the establishment of the federation of the AEF, application of the policy of assimilation was limited to selected local elites, who were accorded citizenship status. The remainder of the population—including some members of the elite—were subject to the *indigenat*, an

Scene depicting the educational and cultural responsibilities of religious education (photo courtesy of the Gabon National Archives).

administrative system that assigned the indigenous population an inferior legal status and gave French administrators wide latitude in governing. Persons under the *indigenat* were subject to penalties and taxation without the legal protection afforded citizens. The abolition of the *indigenat* became a rallying theme for many groups that experienced the abusive practices of this system.

Until 1905, when the exclusive control of education by the Catholic church was ended by anticlerical forces in France, educated Gabonese were the products of a system that illustrated the twin goals of the civilizing mission—the adoption of Christianity and identification of the individual with the form and substance of French civilization. This union of cultural, religious, and military forces created a Gabonese elite attuned to the French presence and subservient to its interests. It was, paradoxically, from this same group that resistance to colonization emerged, in the form of nationalism—but a nationalism that continued a deep commitment to France and French civilization.

In fact, resistance to the Europeans had begun with the first wave of exploration in the fifteenth century. On numerous occasions, most notably the Ndiwa attack on the Dutch in 1600, indigenous groups fought back against the invaders. Bouët's treaties were accompanied by continuing efforts on the part of the French to pacify the local population, and his initial journey on the *Malouine* had been undertaken in part as reprisal for an earlier Mpongwé attack against a French ship. Armed uprisings occurred throughout the nineteenth and early twentieth centuries, although resistance was often geographically restricted and limited by rivalries among the various groups opposing the French. The most serious rebellion was led by the Fang leader Emane Tole, who in 1903 organized a number of Fang clans to resist French control of the middle Ogooué region. Tole was betrayed by rival Fang and defeated by the combined forces of the French army and the private militia of the SHO. Exiled to Grand Bassam in the Ivory Coast, Tole's betrayal by fellow Fang appeared to signal the adoption by the Fang of a fatalistic attitude about the colonial reality. After Tole's exile, the level of rebellion declined; the last major acts of armed resistance took place in 1920, significantly, in Fang areas. Resistance did not, however, come to an end; a few Gabonese formed the core of several organizations that actively pursued the rights of colonized peoples.[26]

The education of the indigenous population—an undertaking primarily of the Catholic church—created a group of Gabonese increasingly differentiated from their compatriots. Along with religion and education, social interaction, including marriage between Europeans and Gabonese, produced an identifiable and favored group, the *métis*, who, along with the commercially active Mpongwé, formed the foundation of a Gabonese elite. Most were educated in Bessieux's mission school or, after 1900, by the Brothers of St. Gabriel at the Ecole Montfort in Libreville and an affiliated institution in Lambaréné. Although anticlerical legislation in France in 1905 severely reduced funding for parochial education, a resurgence took place with the decision by the AEF administration in Brazzaville to restore funding to the religious schools. The few public schools created in the aftermath of the church-state separation were poor substitutes and did not receive adequate financial support until the conclusion of World War II.

In the years after World War I, children of wealthy *métis* and Mpongwé continued their education in France, where they were exposed to the themes of liberalism and democracy prominent in postwar Europe. Gabonese who served in the French army during the war were also less than enthusiastic about the state of affairs in the colonies. In France and in French Africa, serious discussion began about the future of the peoples that France had gathered in its empire.

The first concerted voices of Gabonese anticolonialism appeared in the pages of *L'Echo gabonais*, a monthly newspaper published by two expatriate Gabonese, Louis Bigmann and Laurent Antchouey, in Dakar and, later, as *La Voix coloniale*, in Nice. Bigmann and Antchouey, both veterans of World War I, were associated with Jeunesse gabonaise (JG), Gabon's first indigenous political organization, and the Ligue des droits de l'homme et du citoyen (LDHC), an anticolonialist group active in a number of colonial territories in the postwar period. In Gabon, the leadership of both organizations drew extensively on educated Mpongwé in the Libreville region. Throughout the 1920s, with the support of the LDHC and contributors in the Mpongwé community, *L'Echo gabonais* and *La Voix coloniale* were persistent voices for reform of the colonial system. Antchouey died in 1926, the victim of an accidental drowning, but Bigmann eventually returned to Gabon and in the postindependence era served several terms as president of the National Assembly.

Rivalry among the estuary groups weakened their effectiveness in the anticolonial movement. In 1926, François-de-Paul Vane formed the Mutuelle gabonaise, expressing Mpongwé opposition to *métis* accorded a privileged status by the French authorities. The creation of the Amicale des métis and other efforts on the part of Mpongwé to organize prompted the politicization of Fang clans and the creation of the Comité des intérêts pahouins, an organization that provided the first significant expression of Fang political interests and concerns about colonial affairs. Estuary Fang particularly resented the favored status of the influential Mpongwé and *métis*, and it grew increasingly clear that the estuary population, historically dominated by Mpongwé, feared the challenge posed by the Fang newcomers. Distinctions among the political parties of the country reflected the ethnic divisions of the estuary and the apprehension among the non-Fang groups of the estuary over their traditional privileges.[27] Calls for reform of the colonial system continued, but it was the advent of World War II that brought about the first serious and systematic review of the colonial system and consideration of its future. The Brazzaville conference called by de Gaulle in 1944 was the occasion for an important discussion about a process designed to liberalize France's African empire.

WORLD WAR II AND INDEPENDENCE

Motivating the conference in Brazzaville was the need to unify the empire to defeat Germany. In the early period of the war, the empire was in turmoil. Supporters of de Gaulle's government in exile in London fought battles throughout Africa with forces of the Vichy regime of Marshal Philippe Pétain. In Gabon, Vichy received considerable support from the French who controlled the economic life of the colony and Gabon's conservative clergy, led by the bishop of Libreville, Monsignor Louis Tardy. Within the AEF and the larger framework of French Africa, Gabon's *colons* were among the staunchest supporters of the Vichy regime. Efforts by de Gaulle's supporters in the West and Equatorial African federations to rally support for the Free French cause were not well received in Libreville (and discrimination against the colony of Gabon by the postwar AEF administration in Brazzaville was an important legacy of the war years). After a number of encounters, Free French forces commanded by Colonel Philippe Leclerc captured Libreville on November 8, 1940, and the economic capital, Port Gentil, several days later. By December 1940, Free French forces controlled all the member colonies of the AEF and assigned management of the administrative apparatus of the federation to the de Gaulle loyalist Félix Eboué, a career administrator born in the French colony of Guyana; Eboué thus became the first black administrator in the colonial service to achieve the rank of governor-general.

The Brazzaville conference was attended by representatives from all the colonies in French Africa. De Gaulle established the tone of the conference in a major address in which he outlined a participatory role for the colonies in a proposed French Community. No mention was made at this time, at least by de Gaulle, of the idea of self-determination; rather, the conference established the authority of the Free French government in the empire and laid a foundation for a dialogue that would extend into the 1950s. Significantly, the conference—and de Gaulle—supported the ideas of Governor-General Eboué on a number of matters of immediate importance to the colonies.

Eboué proposed abolition of the policy of assimilation, arguing that it was unnecessary to recast African society in a European mold. He argued that effective and efficient government required gaining the cooperation of the indigenous elites, and to this end, he pursued an array of policies intended to enhance the role, status, and privileges of local elites in the federation. During his tenure as governor-general, which was curtailed by his death in late 1944, he sponsored measures to maintain the integrity of local cultures and increased the number of African civil servants in the colonial apparatus, granting several hundred persons a special elite status that exempted them from the restraints of the *indigenat*. In the area of education, *écoles supérieures* (secondary schools) were instituted in each of the territories of the federation—the first advanced public schools in French Africa.[28]

The period following World War II was the most significant era in the formation of Gabon's elite as well as for the political evolution of French Africa. In 1956, in the spirit of the Brazzaville conference, the French National Assembly passed the *loi cadre*, a radical departure from colonial governance. Discussed at Brazzaville in 1944, the *loi cadre* implemented de Gaulle's promise of a participatory role for the colonies within the framework of a French Community modeled generally on the British Commonwealth. The *loi cadre* is best understood as enabling legislation that authorized representative assemblies in both the West and Equatorial African federations. In a national referendum in 1946, French voters had agreed to de Gaulle's proposal for representation of the African territories in the French National Assembly; previously, African representation had been limited to the four special communes of Senegal. In according the franchise to African voters, the referendum also brought an end to the restrictive policies of the infamous *indigenat*.

Expanding African representation in the French National Assembly effectively structured the debate about the future of the French empire in terms that reflected the French ideological spectrum. For some time, the leading African voices took their cues from their ideological partners in the legislature. In the debates, Léopold Sédar Senghor of Senegal and Félix Houphouët-Boigny of the Ivory Coast reflected the conflict between their nationalist sentiments and the impact of French culture and civilization on their intellectual and political development; both men played pivotal roles in the direction and tone of the political debate that began in earnest with the passage of the *loi cadre*.

Prior to the *loi cadre*, the colonial service provided the only real opportunity for Africans to participate in public affairs. Policymaking was the exclusive prerogative of French administrators selected by the government in Paris. The new Territorial Assembly provided an arena in which Gabonese politicians could discuss economic and political issues from a perspective that differed from that of French administrators and *colons* who monopolized the affairs of the colony. Indeed, both the tone and substance of the postindependence Gabonese political debate took shape initially in the assembly. It is important to note, as well, that the bitter rivalry between the two most significant figures in postindependence politics, Jean-Hilaire Aubame and Léon Mba, originated in the chambers of the Territorial Assembly.

Aubame was the most well known Gabonese political figure. An associate of Eboué's in Brazzaville, his achievements in various administrative assignments made him one of the most respected public figures in French Africa. It was this prominence that led to his selection as the first representative to the French National Assembly after the 1946 referendum. Aubame served as the deputy from the Middle Congo (Gabon and Congo-Brazzaville) from 1946 until the end of the Fourth Republic in 1958. Throughout his career, Aubame remained active in Fang affairs in the Woleu N'Tem, the center of the Fang population in Gabon and the political base of his organization, the Union démocratique et sociale gabonaise (UDSG). The UDSG maintained an affiliation throughout this period with the Parti du régroupement africain (PRA) of Léopold Senghor of Senegal. Although the position of the PRA and its national affiliates, including Aubame's UDSG, shifted over the next few years, Aubame consistently followed Senghor's lead on questions of reform and change within French Africa. The issue of reform became a critical one in the years following the passage of the *loi cadre* in 1956.

Léon Mba was Aubame's major competitor and the eventual winner in the contest for political power. A Fang from the estuary region, Mba began a long and controversial political career with efforts to improve the status of the estuary Fang. In the estuary Fang community, he acquired a reputation as an expert in customary law. Often called upon to resolve disputes within and among clans, he became an influential figure in Fang society, and in 1924 the French administration appointed him as *chef de canton* (canton chief) in Libreville's Fang quarter—a position well suited for the development of a political constituency. Mba did not remain in the good graces of the French administration, however. In his role as *chef de canton*, he often represented persons in conflict with the French adminis-tration, and his involvement with radical anticolonialist groups was not well received by the French. Mba was also involved with a controversial religious sect, Bwiti, that was perceived by some Fang leaders as a cohesive element in communities experiencing the destabilizing effects of the colonial system. Mba's efforts to solicit support among the Fang were furthered by the devastating effects of the economic crisis of the early 1930s on Fang communities.

Mba's association with Bwiti was considered subversive by French civil administrators, who perceived Bwiti as a possible foundation for a potential Fang challenge to their secular rule; the French clergy viewed Bwiti as a direct threat to their religious authority. In 1933, after several minor encounters with the administration, Mba was arrested on charges arising from the deaths of two Fang women in a Bwiti ceremony. After a spectacular trial, involving charges of ritual murder and cannibalism, Mba was convicted and imprisoned in Ubangi-Shari for three years. After his release, he spent ten years as a civil servant in Brazzaville.

Returning to Libreville in 1946, Mba restored his contacts in the estuary Fang community and several anticolonial groups. He was instru-mental in the creation of the Comité mixte gabonais (CMG), a political party based in the Fang clans of the estuary, inspired by the Rassemble-ment démocratique africain (RDA), an inter-African organization with ties to the French Communist party, led by Houphouët-Boigny of the Ivory Coast. Mba and a number of estuary Fang associated for a time, as well, with the Groupe d'études communistes (GEC), an organization composed primarily of French civil servants appointed to the colonial administration during the prewar Popular Front era and generally sympathetic to the anticolonialist themes of the French left. The French administration banned the GEC in 1947, providing the impetus for organizing the CMG.

During this period of intense political activity, Mba succeeded in reestablishing his credibility among a number of Fang groups. At the Fang congress at Mitzic in 1947, Mba emerged as an important leader with a significant following among Fang groups in several regions of Gabon. Over the next few years, he moderated his militant stance, carefully nurturing a reputation among a broader spectrum of Gabonese as responsible. Mba included French citizens in his political entourage and "tactfully," as noted by Virginia Thompson and Richard Adloff in their 1960 survey of former colonies, added a Frenchwoman to the CMG slate of candidates contesting the Libreville city council elections in 1956.[29] Initially sympathetic to Aubame, Mba now distanced himself, charging that Aubame was only narrowly interested in the welfare of the Fang in the northern Woleu N'Tem. Mba's competition with Aubame continued in the parliamentary elections of 1951 and 1956, when Mba opposed Aubame's bids for reelection to the French National Assembly. Although Mba failed on both occasions, he himself was elected mayor of Libreville in 1956 and used the position to broaden his base of political support. Aligning himself with non-Fang groups, he effectively countered the charge that he was exclusively concerned with promoting Fang interests.

The most significant of Mba's new alliances was with the influential Mpongwé politician, Paul Gondjout, with whose assistance Mba opposed Aubame in the Territorial Assembly and the elections to the French National Assembly. Since the early 1950s, Gondjout had actively opposed Aubame; in his eyes, and those of the non-Fang estuary elite, Aubame represented a real threat to their traditional hegemony. In 1954, Mba and Gondjout joined forces in the newly created Bloc démocratique gabonais (BDG), a move that cemented their relationship and, significantly, extended Mba's political base in the influential Mpongwé community. Mba's alliance with Gondjout was facilitated by the RDA's break with the French Communist party in 1951 and Mba's decision to move toward a more conservative stance. The association thus served both Gondjout's avowed goal of developing a political movement that was not based on tribalism, and Mba's efforts to acquire a more moderate, conciliatory image.

In 1957, after several unsuccessful efforts to unseat Aubame, the Mba-Gondjout alliance again contested Aubame's UDSG in elections for the Territorial Assembly. With substantial financial assistance from French timber interests and wealthy Mpongwé businesspersons from Libreville, the BDG candidates, including Mba and Gondjout, succeeded in electing a substantial BDG contingent to the assembly. Although Aubame's party won a majority of popular votes, the legislative districts were gerrymandered to benefit BDG candidates. Following the election, Mba became vice president of the Government Council (the lieutenant governor was nominally the president) and the BDG dominated the legislature and controlled a majority of the cabinet positions. This victory was clearly a high point in Mba's career to date and the foundation for his future efforts to eliminate Aubame and monopolize political power. It was during this period, probably due to his alliance with Gondjout, that Mba received the support of influential French timber merchants such as Roland Bru, who became one of Mba's most important supporters and a key figure in maintaining French influence during the Mba era.[30]

Throughout the postwar period, the competition between Aubame and Mba, and to a limited extent, Gondjout, reflected the struggle for power among distinctly different interests. Aubame represented the important Fang community of the Woleu N'Tem and was generally supported by the French administration and the Roman Catholic leadership. A practicing Catholic, he was viewed as a political moderate, in contrast to Mba, whose association with the Communist-linked GEC and the religious sect Bwiti undermined his credibility with the French establishment. It is noteworthy that the two leading political figures in Gabon at this time were Fang. By the 1930s, the Fang were the largest group in Gabon and the exclusive occupants of the prosperous northern region of the Woleu N'Tem. Their continuing migration southward challenged the traditional Mpongwé dominance in the estuary region. Postwar politics in Gabon reflected Fang concern about their economic and political position vis-à-vis the older estuary groups and, in the animosity between Aubame and Mba, differences between the *évolués* (westernized) Fang of the estuary and the more traditional Fang of the agricultural Woleu N'Tem. Although both Aubame and Mba were committed to advancing Fang interests, it became increasingly apparent that they held divergent views on a number of critical subjects. But on the question of Gabon's status within the framework of the French colonial empire, Mba and Aubame expressed surprising agreement, and the competition between Aubame and Mba was temporarily postponed when events in France and Algeria opened a new era for the French colonies in Africa.

Gabon's accession to independence occurred as a direct result of the Algerian revolution and the shock waves from this event that upset the equilibrium of the French colonial system. De Gaulle's return to power in 1958 led to the dissolution of the Union française and the legal ties that bound the colonies to the metropolis. Within two years of the birth of the French Fifth Republic, Gabon and the other colonies of France's African empire were independent. Ironically, Gabon acquired independence without an overwhelming national mandate or the support of its two most prominent political figures, for throughout the debate on the future of France's relationship with its colonies, Mba and Aubame favored a continuing association with France. In fact, during the preindependence era, Aubame and Mba expressed the view that complete independence from

France might not be in the best interests of the Gabonese. Both initially supported Gabon's acquiring a status like that of Guadeloupe or Martinique, with total integration into the French system of overseas administrative units. Although proposed in the early discussions, the idea was dropped as events dictated a more dramatic conclusion.

In 1958, in the wake of Dien Bien Phu, with civil war imminent over its Algerian policy, the French government—that is, de Gaulle—offered the colonies an opportunity to express their preference for the future in the form of a referendum designed to gauge the level of support for membership in a French Community resembling the British Commonwealth. In the 1958 referendum, an overwhelming number of Gabonese, including a substantial number of French nationals, voted for continued association with France. What opposition there was—the vote was 190,334 to 15,244—was organized by René-Paul Sousatte and Jean-Jacques Boucavel, founders of the Parti d'union nationale gabonaise (whose acronym, PUNGA, is the Eshira word for tempest). PUNGA was composed primarily of Eshira and Bapounou from the southern regions who resented the Fang-Mpongwé dominance of Gabonese politics and used the occasion to express these regional grievances.

Following the referendum, French Africa was in a state of flux. Guinean voters, endorsing the position of the nationalist leader Sékou Touré, voted overwhelmingly for independence, and strong proindependence sentiments existed in Niger and Cameroon. The French acceptance of Guinea's decision and their abrupt, destabilizing withdrawal from the country signaled a fundamental change in assumptions about the future. Algeria's independence, along with France's decision to grant independence to Morocco and Tunisia, demonstrated French willingness to accept a rupture with their colonies. The end was in sight when Houphouët-Boigny and Senghor failed in their efforts to establish a federated relationship. It was, in fact, the move of the Ivory Coast to request independence that effectively brought the colonial era in French Africa to an end. Houphouët-Boigny was a champion of the idea of association, and his decision to request total independence for the Ivory Coast marked the end of an era. Although the Gabonese voted for membership in the French Community, they showed no appreciable support for participation in a renewed federation of equatorial African states in an association with France. Gabon had long played the role of bridesmaid in the AEF, and the Gabonese agreed in opposing any political arrangement that might again subordinate them to their old federation partners.[31] Following a period of internal autonomy granted by the French National Assembly in 1958, on August 17, 1960, Léon Mba, vice president of the Government Council, became the prime minister of an independent Republic of Gabon. With an uneasy truce established between Mba and Aubame, many of the prominent figures in the preindependence debate joined the government.

NOTES

1. Frédéric Meyo-Bibang, *Aperçu historique du Gabon* (Libreville: Institut pedagogique national, 1973); and *Le Gabon* (Paris: Hatier, 1975). The latter work is a very uneven elementary school text.

2. Cheikh Anta Diop, *Pre-Colonial Black Africa* (Westport, Conn.: Lawrence Hill, 1987), pp. 212–234.

3. Banjakila Bakajika, "Les ancêtres des Bantu vivaient-ils au Tchad ou au Shaba?" *Afrique histoire*, no. 9 (1983), pp. 17–22.

4. The discovery at Ikengué and the tremendous burdens of archaeological research in Gabon are discussed in Lazare Digombe, Michel Locko, and James Emejulu, "Nouvelles recherches archeologiques à Ikengué (Fernan Vaz, Province de l'Ogooué-Maritime, Gabon): Un site datant de 1300 B.C.," *L'anthropologie* (Paris), vol. 91, no. 2 (1987), pp. 705–710.

5. Elikia M'Bokolo, *Noirs et blancs en Afrique équatoriale: Les sociétés Côtières et la pénétration française vers 1820–1874* (Paris: Mouton, 1981), particularly Chapters 1–4.

6. Karl David Patterson, *The Northern Gabon Coast to 1875* (Oxford: Clarendon Press, 1975), Chapters 1–3. This region is also discussed by Henry H. Bucher, "The Mpongwé of the Gabon Estuary," Ph.D. diss., University of Wisconsin–Madison, 1977.

7. It remains difficult, however, to assess the impact and significance of gender on the social patterns of the era. Matrilineal traditions among the Orungu gave women a significant, albeit passive, role in the determination of clan leadership; in his study of the era, Elikia M'Bokolo noted that Mpongwé women participated as equals in discussion of clan affairs, although formal positions of authority were monopolized by men. Additionally, some Mpongwé women were designated as free women, placing them in the social hierarchy between slaves and free men, entitling them to supervise the work of the slaves but not allowing them entry into the exclusive group of *courtiers* who engaged in the lucrative intermediary commerce with the Europeans. The advent of commerce did, however, prompt a new status for some Mpongwé women. According to M'Bokolo, the clans considered marriage between women of their clan and Europeans to be of substantial benefit to the clan. Thus, those women determined by the clan elders to be eligible for such marriages acquired a privileged status within the clan (M'Bokolo, *Noirs et blancs en Afrique équatoriale*, p. 24). The acquisition of status as a function of relationships with Europeans was an important consequence of increasing contacts between Europeans and Gabonese.

8. André Raponda-Walker and Roger Sillans, *Rites et croyances des peuples du Gabon* (Paris: Présence africaine, 1962). Raponda-Walker's major work on the nineteenth century is *Notes d'histoire du Gabon* (Montpellier: Institut d'études centrafricaines, 1960).

9. Joseph Ambouroue-Avaro, *Un peuple gabonais à l'aube de la colonisation* (Paris: Editions Karthala, 1981), pp. 33–88.

10. Raponda-Walker and Sillans, *Rites et croyances,* pp. 11–167.

11. M'Bokolo, *Noirs et blancs en Afrique équatoriale,* pp. 23–28.

12. This era is discussed by several authors; the most helpful are Ange Ratanga-Atoz, *Initiation à l'histoire générale du Gabon* (Libreville: Ministère de l'éducation nationale/Univérsité Omar Bongo, 1979); and Nicolas Metegue-N'Nah, *Economies et sociétés au Gabon dans la première moitié du XXeme siècle* (Paris: Harmattan, 1979).

13. For a discussion of slavery in Gabon, see Patterson, *The Northern Gabon Coast to 1875,* pp. 26–47.

14. Raponda-Walker, *Notes d'histoire du Gabon,* pp. 23–29.

15. Elikia M'Bokolo, *Le roi Denis: La première tentative de modernisation du Gabon* (Dakar: Nouvelles éditions africaines, 1976), pp. 9–12.

16. M'Bokolo, *Noirs et blancs en Afrique équatoriale,* pp. 29–31.

17. Ministère de la France d'outre-mer, *Traité conclu en 1846, entre le Capitaine de Vaisseau E. Bouët-Willaumez, commandant la Frégate le Caraibe et les Rois et Chefs du Gabon,* Gabon National Archives, Libreville (translation by the author).

18. There are several works on the early years of French colonization in Gabon; the most useful are Nicolas Metegue-N'Nah, *L'implantation coloniale au Gabon: Résistance d'un peuple,* vol. 1 (Paris: Harmattan, 1981); and Hubert Deschamps, "Quinze ans de Gabon: Les débuts de l'établissement français, 1839–1853," *Revue d'histoire d'outre mer,* vol. 50, no. 180–181 (1965).

19. M'Bokolo, *Noirs et blanc en Afrique équatoriale,* pp. 130–131.

20. For an excellent discussion of this era and the evolution of French policy, see Bernard Schnapper, *La politique et le commerce français dans la golfe du Guinée de 1838 à 1871* (Paris: Mouton, 1961), pp. 135–138.

21. For the colonial era, see chapters by Henri Brunschwig, "French Exploration in Tropical Africa from 1865–1898," and Catherine Coquery-Vidrovitch, "French Colonization in Africa to 1920: Administration and Development," in P. Duignan, and L. H. Gann, eds., *The History and Politics of Colonialism, 1870–1914* (London: Cambridge University Press, 1969).

22. Ange Ratanga-Atoz, "Commerce, economie et société dans le Gabon du XIXeme–début XXeme siècle," *Annales de l'école nationale d'administration* (Libreville), 2 (1977), pp. 85–96.

23. For detailed accounts of the events and major figures of this era, see Metegue-N'Nah, *L'implantation coloniale au Gabon,* pp. 59–101; D. Bruce Marshall, *The French Colonial Myth and Constitution-Making in the Fourth Republic* (New Haven, Conn.: Yale University Press, 1973), pp. 42–74; and John P. Hargreaves, *Prelude to the Partition of West Africa* (New York: St. Martin's Press, 1970), pp. 145–252.

24. For a discussion of the concessionary era, see Catherine Coquery-Vidrovitch, *Le Congo au temps des grandes compagnies concessionaires, 1898–1930* (Paris: Mouton, 1972); and by the same author, "French Colonization in Africa to 1920,"

25. Cited in Ronald Segal, *African Profiles* (New York: Penguin Books, 1962), p. 176.

26. For an overview of Gabonese resistance to colonialism, see Metegue-N'Nah, *L'implantation coloniale au Gabon,* pp. 63–107.

27. For a discussion of the emergence of a Fang political consciousness, see Georges Balandier, *Sociologie actuelle de l'Afrique noire: Dynamique sociale en Afrique centrale* (Paris: Quadrige/Presses universitaire de France, 1982), Part 2, Chapters 1–3.

28. For Eboué's policies, see Félix Eboué, *La nouvelle politique indigène* (Brazzaville: Afrique française libre, 1941). For a biography of Eboué, see Brian Weinstein, *Eboué* (New York: Oxford University Press, 1971).

29. For discussions of this era, see Balandier, *Sociologie actuelle de l'Afrique noire*, Chapter 3; and Virginia Thompson and Richard Adloff, *The Emerging States of Equatorial Africa* (Stanford, Calif.: Stanford University Press, 1960), Chapter 22.

30. The most informative and accurate account of this period is Gilbert Comte, "La république gabonaise: Treize années d'histoire," *Revue française d'études politiques africaines*, 90 (June 1973), pp. 39–57.

31. There is an excellent analysis of this period in Patrick Manning, *Francophone Sub-Saharan Africa, 1880–1985* (New York: Cambridge University Press, 1988), pp. 57–62 for Gabon and central Africa.

2

The Postindependence Era

Constitutionally, the newly independent Gabonese Republic was a mirror image of France. The administrative organization of the state reflected the centralized traditions of the metropole and patterns and habits of political activity demonstrated the acquired culture of French politics. According to some observers, Gabon had been the most franco-phile of all the French possessions. Gabon's leaders prided themselves on their amicable relationships with their former colonial overlords, and life in the capital city of Libreville was described as one of easy camaraderie between the French and the Gabonese. Transformed by the process of independence from *colons* into citizens of an independent republic, many French residents of the country continued their lives without any percep-tible changes. Fundamentally, nothing had changed. Gabon acquired the form of independence, leaving the critical power of decisionmaking about foreign affairs and economic matters largely in the hands of French former colonial administrators, who in many cases became functionaries in the new government or representatives of French ministries with interests in Gabon. The offical relationship between France and Gabon was shaped by a set of accords that defined French prerogatives and thus the param-eters of Gabonese independence. France continued to play a predominant role in Gabonese affairs as the newly emergent Gabonese nation struggled with the challenge of independence.

THE LÉON MBA ERA: 1960–1967

Gabon's peaceful accession to independence augured a successful national future. Although the truce between Aubame and Mba was increasingly strained, it appeared that the governing system that existed at the time could keep their rivalry in check. In retrospect, it is clear that Mba was intent on developing a regime that mirrored his personal goals. From the moment of independence to the modification of the constitution in 1963, Mba moved to eliminate his rivals and all effective opposition to his personal rule.

President Léon Mba (photo courtesy of the Gabon National Archives).

At the time of independence, Gabon employed a classic parliamentary system in which an executive officer—the prime minister—represented a majority coalition in the unicameral national legislature. In the newly formed National Assembly, Mba presided over a coalition government that included Gondjout and other members of the BDG, as well as Aubame and some of his UDSG followers. Mba's appeal for a government of national unity was effective: Many of those who had formerly opposed him—PUNGA leaders Sousatte and Boucavel, for example—rallied to Mba's call for national cooperation. This era of good feeling ended in 1961 when Mba called for a constitutional convention to consider a presidential system like that of France's newly created Fifth Republic, with an enhanced role for the chief executive. Under the existing parliamentary arrangement, Mba was forced to share power with the assembly and, on numerous occasions, to bear opposition criticism of his policies. His reliance on French administrators was often attacked; the more nationalistically minded members of the National Assembly strongly objected to the inclusion of such figures as Roland Bru in the administration. Although Mba responded to these criticisms with a policy called *gabonisation*, that is, the appointment of Gabonese nationals to important administrative positions, his efforts were hindered by the shortage of trained personnel and pressure from the French to retain their structure of influence.

Gondjout was an early victim of Mba's move to consolidate power. Like Aubame and other major political personalities of the period, Gondjout was committed to a multiparty parliamentary system resembling that of the French Fourth Republic. Following independence in 1960, Gondjout and Aubame appeared to represent a broadly based consensus favoring the Gabonese parliamentary system. Both issued reports reinforcing Aubame's statement to the assembly in October 1960 that the principal function of the legislature was to "control the government," the essence of parliamentary politics. It soon became apparent that Mba was not a party to this view. Emphasizing the need for stability— the classic rationale of those who fear the potential *immobilisme* of multiparty parliamentary regimes—Mba stated at the time that a multiparty system would add considerably "to confusion, to anarchy and to disorder" and produce a "dispersion of authority" inherently harmful to the functions of government.[1] In the simplest terms, and clearly reminiscent of de Gaulle's sharp criticism of the institutions of the Fourth Republic, Mba viewed the office of president of the republic as the central institution of his proposed constitution.

As president of the National Assembly, Gondjout organized a censure motion against his old ally, opposing the attempt to transform the parliamentary system into an instrument of Mba's personal rule. Accused of a plot against Mba, Gondjout was arrested, convicted, and sentenced to two years in prison despite the supposed parliamentary immunity from civil or criminal charges. These actions against Gondjout were ratified by the directorate of the BDG in an executive session convened by Mba. A month following Gondjout's conviction and the expulsion of several other BDG members, Mba was elected to Gondjout's previous position as secretary-general of the BDG. Mba then attempted to neutralize his other rivals. Aubame was appointed to the presidency of the Supreme Court, and Sousatte, arrested with Gondjout in 1961 for his opposition to Mba, received an appointment as minister of Agriculture, an essentially symbolic post. Upon his release from prison, Gondjout was appointed to chair the Economic and Social Council, an advisory body on economic and social issues, effectively keeping him from active involvement in the affairs of the government or legislature.

Aubame remained the primary threat to Mba's ambitions. Following the traditional French practice of holding multiple positions—*cumul des positions*—he retained his legislative seat while serving as president of the

Supreme Court. Mba proposed a law that would prohibit the holding of a ministerial position by a deputy in the National Assembly; he assumed Aubame would choose to maintain the more prestigious and financially rewarding position on the court. Although Mba was unable to mobilize the entire BDG to vote for this poorly disguised effort to neutralize Aubame, the law narrowly passed the assembly (Aubame's UDSG voted with a number of BDG members in opposition). In an astute political move that effectively nullified Mba's maneuvering, Aubame chose to retain his seat in the legislature—a decision that infuriated Mba and enhanced Aubame's reputation as a selfless leader.

In spite of Aubame's continuing opposition, Mba succeeded in transforming the system to his design, giving him firm control of the BDG and the National Assembly. Under extraordinary pressure from Mba, the BDG-controlled legislature passed a constitutional amendment creating the position of president of the republic. In the style of the constitution of the French Fifth Republic, the president was to be elected by direct popular vote, and the legislature was relegated to a consultative role. Mba's actions throughout this period create a sense of déjà vu, his efforts to restructure the institutions of Gabonese politics so closely replicating de Gaulle's initiatives in France, climaxing with the adoption of the de Gaulle–inspired presidency of the Gabonese republic.

The period between 1960 and 1964 was a critical one for the fledgling Gabonese state. Mba's efforts to neutralize his major opponents, Aubame and Gondjout, were accompanied by other restrictions. Fearful of the open political debate and competition of a multiparty system, Mba and the legislature became openly repressive. The National Assembly, urged on by the president, curtailed political demonstrations and severely limited freedom of speech and political assembly. One after another of the institutions and habits of democratic politics nurtured in the period of the Territorial Assembly were being destroyed.

In early 1964, Mba made his long-awaited move to implement a one-party state. Using the extraordinary powers of the constitution, he dissolved the National Assembly on January 16 and called elections for February 23. This final effort to achieve uncontested power provoked protest from opposition groups and, more significantly, from a group of young army officers who instigated a coup d'état on the evening of February 17. The coup was not a total surprise. Albert Bernard Bongo, serving at this time as Mba's *directeur de cabinet* (chief of staff), heard about unusual movements in the Libreville barracks and informed Mba, who ignored the report to his detriment, at least for the short term.

The coup was led by young army officers in the Libreville military district who arrested Mba and, according to his later account of events, placed him in detention, initially near Kango in the estuary region and later at Lambaréné, several hours from Libreville.[2] Within hours of the coup, a provisional government led by Aubame and including Gondjout and other leading opposition figures, assumed control, giving the impression to some that they were involved in the planning and execution of the coup. Approximately twenty-four hours later, French paratroopers from bases in Dakar and Brazzaville commanded by General Kergavarat intervened to restore Mba to office. The French moved quickly, and all effective military resistance to the intervention collapsed within several days. Released from detention, Mba returned to office under the protection of the French military. Relatively short-lived but violent reactions to the French move took place in Libreville and Port Gentil, and demonstrations occurred throughout the country in support of the coup, but within a month of his overthrow, Mba had reestablished his authority, and the participants in the coup and the provisional government were in prison.

The French government justified its intervention as a legitimate response to a request by the Mba government for assistance under the terms of a mutual defense pact concluded at the time of Gabon's independence. Mba explained that Vice President Paul-Marie Yembit requested assistance from the French ambassador, Paul Cousseran, who relayed the request to Paris. This account is disputed; it appears that Yembit was, in fact, at Moussambou in the company of U.S. Ambassador Charles Darlington, and the Gabonese minister of Education, Vincent de Paul Nyonda, attending the opening of a primary school built by U.S. Peace Corps volunteers and unaware of events in Libreville until after the intervention began. In his book on the period, Darlington accused the French of an outright betrayal of Gabonese independence; Darlington saw the intervention as a unilateral action on the part of a government in Paris exclusively concerned with its strategic interests. The French action was not without precedent. In 1963, French troops intervened in Togo following the assassination of Sylvanus Olympio, and in the Congo following the fall of Fulbert Youlou. French troops had also been dispatched to Dahomey (Benin) after Hubert Maga's fall from power. Although the circumstances differed in each case, de Gaulle had certainly put former French Africa on notice that France would intervene if it considered its interests in jeopardy. De Gaulle's personal affection for Mba may have also contributed to the French decision.[3]

The French claim of legality is weak. Although international law countenances intervention authorized by mutual agreement, the requested party is not obligated to intervene. Darlington's argument that the intervention was primarily an act of national self-interest on the part of the French seems persuasive. France's nuclear establishment relied on Gabonese uranium, and friendly relations with the Mba government assured the French a strategically important and secure base in central Africa. The

French move itself became an important precedent for Gabonese politics
in that it established the dependence of an unpopular Gabonese regime
on the French military, openly—even conspicuously—garrisoned near the
Libreville airport.[4]

The period following the attempted coup was one of recrimination
and punishment. Aubame received a twenty-year sentence of internment
and hard labor. Those officers who were not killed in the fighting with
the French received long prison terms, and the participants in the short-
lived provisional government received sentences of ten to twenty years.
Gondjout was tried but acquitted; no evidence presented at his trial
substantiated the charge of his involvement in the planning or the imple-
mentation of the coup. Was the exoneration of Gondjout but not Aubame,
simply an illustration of Mba's indebtedness to Gondjout and the importance of the Myéné connection in Mba's plans? Aubame claimed during
his trial that his involvement was after the fact and that his decision to
join the provisional government was in the best interests of the nation
during a moment of crisis. Whatever the truth, here was a tempting
opportunity for Mba to rid himself of his oldest and most dangerous
opponent.

The causes of the coup are disputed. An extraordinary memorandum
from Captain Joachim Pallard of the French military staff to Mba provides
a unique perspective on the events that led to the coup. In an exceptionally
candid confidential report, Pallard outlined factors that in his estimation
created a climate that made the coup likely and, more important, acceptable
among a significant number of Gabonese. Pallard stated it would be an
error to blame the young officers who implemented the "mutiny." The
true causes of the affair were to be found in the "political milieu"; the
officers commanding the rebellious troops were merely "executing policies
determined by the politicians." The essence of Pallard's report was that
the Mba government was perceived as tolerating corruption and even
aiding in the distribution of the nation's wealth to a few avaricious persons
who were acquiring tremendous wealth at the expense of all. The situation
was particularly appalling, Pallard reported to Mba, in a government that
proudly stated it was "by the people and for the people." Pallard raised
such sensitive subjects as bureaucratic abuses, nepotism, and ethnic
favoritism in both the national government and the municipal bureaucracy
in Libreville. In a particularly sharp passage, Pallard cited the pattern of
abuses in the provincial governments, several of which he described as
family preserves devoid of merit.[5]

Pallard's report reinforced the charge that the Mba government was
out of touch with an important segment of Gabonese opinion, in Pallard's
eyes, to its discredit. He concluded that the coup attempt was in large
measure a consequence of the policies of the Mba government and should

not have come as a surprise. In the final paragraph of his report, Pallard apologized to the president (and unidentified "Messieurs"—presumably cabinet members) for his frank criticism of the government and some of its ministerial figures.

The attempted coup brought into focus long-simmering issues of power and authority. Mba had retained a cadre of French advisers and kept the top ranks of the Gabonese administration filled with holdovers from the colonial bureaucracy. Influential former *colons* like Roland Bru reportedly dictated the economic policies of the government, and Mba's recently acquired pro-French attitude created strains in his relationship with the legislature over undue French influence in the affairs of state. In addition, Mba's authoritarian style and his obsession in his first years of governance with eradicating any opposition increased his reliance on his French supporters, many of whom arrogantly considered Gabon their private domain. Gondjout's growing disenchantment with Mba and the disaffection of a number of prominent Mpongwé in the BDG removed the best educated and trained elements of the Gabonese population from active or willing participation in the government. Mba's decision in 1961 to imprison such a previously staunch supporter as Gondjout created the appearance of a vendetta against the traditional Mpongwé elite by the Fang outsider, a perception underscored by an unfortunate physical attack by members of Mba's estuary-based Essoke clan on the venerable Raponda-Walker after he had spoken out against Mba's repressive policies. As time went on, Mba relied ever more on his French supporters, creating the picture of an isolated president propped up in power by the former colonial masters. The intervention of French paratroopers to return Mba to power after the events of February 1964 could only reinforce that image.

Mba's return to power was hardly triumphant. The imprisonment of Aubame and the other participants in the provisional government failed to end opposition. Following Mba's announcement of elections to replace those postponed because of the coup, a group called the Parti de défense des institutions démocratique (DID), organized by Emile Issembe, sought to rally the remaining opposition to Mba. Issembe, the son of a wealthy Mpongwé businessman, had been active in the GEC and the RDA in the preindependence period. Mba prevailed upon the BDG majority in the National Assembly to reduce the number of seats from sixty-seven to forty-seven; ostensibly a cost-cutting measure, the move also limited the chances of the opposition. In the parliamentary elections held on April 12, Mba's party won only a narrow majority of the popular vote and thirty-one of the forty-seven seats in the National Assembly. The DID's sixteen seats were a moral victory for the opposition and the imprisoned Aubame.

In the end, Mba's efforts to tighten his grip on the institutions of government were enhanced by the attempted coup; the French military intervention dampened a potentially stronger opposition to the regime. Many Gabonese felt constrained to avoid any precipitous action against the Mba regime that might incite a second French military adventure. Nor was the possibility that the intervention may have been a unilateral action on the part of the French lost on many Gabonese. Within a relatively short time, opposition to the regime dissipated, creating a de facto one-party state. Members of the DID were subtly coerced into cooperating with Mba's renewed call for national unity, and by the end of 1964 only a handful of the sixteen DID dissidents in the National Assembly remained in active opposition. Aubame was in prison, and Mba found himself in an enviable situation, with no longer any compelling reason to formally establish a one-party state and possibly generate renewed unrest and a second French military intervention. Supported by a BDG majority in the legislature and a corps of Gabonese and French bureaucrats whose positions depended on their support of the president, he firmly controlled the apparatus of the state and soon acquired from the BDG-controlled legislature extraordinary powers to limit civil liberties.[6]

Although Mba had succeded in monopolizing power, the state of his health raised questions for the future of the Gabonese state. As Mba grew more seriously ill, his vice president and heir apparent, Albert Bernard Bongo, increasingly controlled the affairs of state. The BDG-controlled legislature in 1966 allowed Mba to replace the incumbent vice president Paul-Marie Yembit with Bongo; the constitutional revision of 1963 had implemented a U.S.-style presidential–vice presidential relationship designed to resolve the problem of succession in situations of prolonged illness or the death of the incumbent president. During the final days of his life, Mba was hospitalized in Paris, effectively removed from the politics and intrigues of the succession.

Bongo was the prototype of a new, young group of technocrats whose initiation to politics came in the ranks of the national bureaucracy in Libreville. In a point of historical irony, Bongo came to Mba's attention while serving on Aubame's staff after an administrative apprenticeship in Brazzaville. Bongo acquired a reputation as an effective administrator and during Mba's illness assumed several major governmental responsibilities. Within months of being named *directeur de cabinet*, Bongo acquired the ministerial portfolios of national defense, national planning, information, and tourism. (This was also the moment for the entry into the national administration of other young bureaucrats, such as Georges Rawiri and Léon Mébiame, who would form the next generation of national leadership.) Upon Mba's death in Paris on November 27, 1967, Vice President

Albert Bernard Bongo at age thirty-two became the second president of the Republic of Gabon.

THE BONGO ERA BEGINS:
THE SEARCH FOR ABSOLUTE POWER

Speculation continues about Mba's choice of Bongo as his successor. The most widely held theory proposes that Bongo was the choice of a powerful group of Frenchmen whose influence in Gabon continued without interruption after independence in 1960. This is the view of Pierre Péan who, in his controversial book, *Affaires africaines*, asserted the existence of a *clan des gabonais* composed of key members of the French government and influential Gabonese in alliance with strategically placed French nationals who controlled the economy of Gabon. In this view, the principal actor throughout the ten years following independence was de Gaulle's primary adviser on African affairs, Jacques Foccart. According to Péan, Foccart maintained French control in the former colonies through the *réseau Foccart*, an intricate "network" of persons who, in the case of Gabon, collaborated with the French military and major French economic interests to guarantee access to Gabon's strategic minerals. In Péan's analysis, Bongo was simply an instrument in Foccart's neocolonial system; Péan named former French ambassador and close Mba adviser, Maurice Delauney as a central figure in the Foccart network and as the person who handpicked Bongo as Mba's successor.[7]

A second view emphasizes the paternal relationship between Mba and Bongo, considering the presidency Bongo's reward for loyal, efficient service to his mentor. In fact, the two views are not contradictory or mutually incompatible. Bongo's role as *directeur de cabinet* certainly brought him into close contact with leaders of the French community, and as Mba's condition worsened, Bongo emerged as the most significant Gabonese political figure. It is difficult to believe that Mba's successor did not have at least the tacit approval of key persons in the French community and those officials in Paris, like Foccart, who collaborated closely with the Mba government.

Bongo's accession to the presidency produced dramatic changes in the political climate. He was perceived by many Gabonese as a welcome departure from the Fang-Mpongwé dominance of Gabonese politics. A member of the minority Batéké group, whose population is concentrated around Franceville in the far southern region of the country, Bongo represented a real possibility for national cooperation with political and economic participation by ethnic groups long overwhelmed by the Fang-Mpongwé monopolization of political life.[8]

President El Hadj Omar Bongo (photo courtesy of the Gabon National Archives).

One of Bongo's first presidential acts was to grant amnesty to most of those who participated in the provisional government at the time of the 1964 coup. Aubame was a notable exception to Bongo's policy of clemency. As Mba's most prominent and vigorous opponent, Aubame was a person who could galvanize support against the new regime. Only in 1972 was Aubame released from internment and allowed to leave the country for exile in France. In 1981, after renewed appeals by Bongo for national reconciliation, Aubame, aged sixty-seven, returned to Gabon, and received an honorific appointment as a counselor of state.

Bongo's policy of reconciliation was not a signal for a return to the open parliamentary process preferred by many of Mba's opponents. In fact, Bongo moved aggressively to complete the process of consolidating power begun years before by his predecessor. His major innovation was the dissolution of all political parties and their replacement by a single party, the Parti démocratique gabonais (PDG). Echoing Mba, Bongo argued that multipartyism was inimical to the development of Gabonese nationalism. In his New Year's Day address in 1968, he spoke of the need for a *rénovation nationale* (national renewal) and vowed that politics in Gabon would henceforth involve dialogue and participation. *Rénovation* meant, at least in theory, a decisive step away from the ethnic divisions and rivalries that characterized the past, a mobilization of the full human and physical resources of the country in the formidable task of nation building. According to the new president, there would be an end to rewards for belonging to one or another ethnic group; the emphasis was now on being Gabonese.

Bongo's decision to eliminate opposition parties was accompanied by an important initiative involving the trade unions, which had been active in the preindependence era. Mba had already sought to limit their power during his tenure as president. In 1963, in an encounter described as menacing, Mba met with representatives of the unions and gave them notice to align themselves with the goals of his administration. At an extraordinary congress of the union leadership in Libreville in 1969, Bongo received pledges of support for his policy of renewal, and following his suggestions, the representatives to the congress formed a single organization, the Féderation syndicale gabonaise (FESYGA). After several years of cooperation between FESYGA and the PDG, FESYGA was formally incorporated as a component organization of the governing PDG by government ordinance in July 1973.[9]

Bongo reinforced his call for renewal and national cooperation with a policy of clemency. He initiated an important dialogue with a number of leading exiles, notably Germain Mba in Brazzaville, upon the urging of President Houphouët-Boigny of the Ivory Coast who became an adviser and confidant of his young presidential colleague. Mba, a distant relation of Léon Mba, had resigned his position in Brazzaville as the assistant secretary-general of the Union africaine et malgache to protest the French intervention and organized a group in opposition to the Mba regime, the Mouvement gabonais d'action populaire, which later became the Mouvement de Libération nationale de Gabon. After Aubame, Mba was the leading critic of the government, and his prominence in Brazzaville and francophone Africa made him an embarrassment to the government. With Bongo's call for national reconciliation, Mba returned to Gabon in 1968 and received several major diplomatic assignments, which kept him out of the country while neutralizing him as a potential competitor. Bongo urged all the exiles to return to Gabon and join him in his mission of renewal, and to those who accepted, like Mba, he gave essentially honorific positions in the growing Libreville bureaucracy. In a chilling conclusion to his decision to return to Gabon, Germain Mba was murdered under exceptionally strange circumstances in Libreville in 1971. His body was never recovered and suspicion persists over Bongo's role in the affair.

In another move to bolster his regime and advance the cause of renewal, Bongo included several young army officers in his government, effectively aligning the army with the goals of his administration and implicitly pardoning the army for its involvement in the events of 1964.

Bongo's policy of amnesty and reconciliation relied extensively on Gabon's growing wealth. By the late 1960s, sales of petroleum, uranium, and manganese earned millions of francs for the national treasury. Participation and cooperation were rewarded handsomely, and the president was particularly generous to those who expressed their personal and political allegiance to his regime.

Bongo's decision in 1968 to dissolve the existing political parties and replace them with the PDG was accepted with equanimity by most Gabonese. In actuality, the parties had never evolved beyond the personalities and ambitions of their leaders or established deep organizational or ideological roots in the populace. There is evidence that many Gabonese were simply exhausted by the struggle between Mba and Aubame and resented this personal war. Bongo's policy of national reconciliation, supported by gestures of clemency and magnanimity, appeared to serve his goals. He received overwhelming support for his policies at the first congress of the PDG in 1970. Under his direct leadership and control, the PDG became a cornerstone of Bongo's structure of power.

The PDG was designed to foster the appearance of national unity and stability, the bases of Bongo's appeal to the people of Gabon. By eliminating all formalized opposition and legitimizing only one political organization, Bongo created a monopoly over the decisionmaking process. PDG members held all public offices; a system of patronage, controlled by the secretary-general of the party, rewarded the faithful with attractive sinecures in the civil and military bureaucracies. Bongo's control over the party was assured by his dual role as president of the republic and founder and secretary-general of the PDG. In 1985, Bongo relinquished the office of secretary-general, although he retained the right to determine the holder of the position. His replacement was the longtime prime minister, Léon Mébiame. Although Mébiame and Bongo are often viewed as rivals, Bongo's appointments to the party secretariat appear to keep Mébiame's activities in check. Periodic accounts of Mébiame's failing health suggest that his status in the upper echelons of the regime may be tenuous.

Internal party decisions are reached by a Gabonese variant of Lenin's democratic centralism. Decisionmaking has been the primary responsibility of the Political Bureau, whose members also serve in important government positions, assuring the continuity of policymaking between the party and the government. From the creation of the PDG in 1968 until the reforms of 1990, the key positions of the party without exception were held by the most prominent members of the PDG. With the members of the PDG inner circle and the large ministerial contingent as pieces, Bongo has played an intricate chess game. His policy has been to foster insecurity by creating and removing both cabinet positions and their occupants at will. Gabon's cabinet has included as many as forty-six positions—an unusually large delegation of ministerial responsibilities for a country of Gabon's size. Cabinet members reportedly receive yearly salaries in excess of U.S.$200,000 and deputies to the National Assembly receive monthly salaries of U.S.$3,000. At the next level in the organizational structure, the Central Committee comprises all the members of the Political Bureau and others nominated by the secretary-general for their contributions to the social, economic, and political life of the country. In reality, the Central Committee has usurped the representative role of the National Assembly. Central Committee members represent a broad spectrum of interests— youth, labor, women, and so forth—within the structure of the party; interests not acknowledged by their inclusion are, in effect, negligible or undesirable. This incorporation of many prominent figures and interest groups into the PDG effectively constrains opposition activity. Given the reality that the legislative role is consultative and symbolic, those who wish to make demands on the political system are, of necessity, limited to the internal decisionmaking system of the PDG—or the streets.

In developing this form of corporate representation within the PDG, Bongo shaped a decisionmaking system that depends upon his ability— and resources—to satisfy the variety of demands that characterize a society as diverse as Gabon's. The presence of serious expressions of discontent inside and outside of the country underscore the point that the système Bongo is not perfect, but Bongo has successfully created a structure of power that closely aligns the fortunes of the country with those of its president. In many ways, the PDG has served as a well-organized lobbying group committed to the ambitions of the president of the republic. For many years, Bongo has assiduously cultivated the image of the grand camarad who knows what is best for the country, even coming dangerously close to a cult of personality that places personal power and privilege above the welfare of the state and its citizens.

Within Gabon's carefully balanced institutions are occasional indications that the rhetoric of participation is taken seriously by members of the PDG. They have used the party's annual meetings to express displeasure with the policies of a particular minister and, upon occasion, with the government in general. At the annual meeting in 1979, Bongo took steps to democratize the party after delegates expressed discontent about their limited role in decisionmaking within the party. Representatives to the party congress were permitted to propose more names for positions on the Central Committee than the actual number of seats, allowing members of the party to express their preference for certain candidates. The most immediate result of this modification in party procedure was the embarrassing defeat of Bongo's own directeur de cabinet in his attempt at reelection to the Central Committee. Similar changes were made in the manner of selection of deputies to the National Assembly, and the legislative term of office was reduced from seven to five years. At the third party congress in 1986, the central committee was increased to 297 members, and, significantly, five women were appointed to an enlarged Political Bureau of 44 members. Bongo's appointment of women to the Political Bureau acknowledged the increasing significance of women in public affairs and their role in the PDG. For some time the women's section of the PDG, the Union des Femmes du PDG, has provided the party with an extraordinary injection of energy, and Bongo appears to have strong electoral support from women throughout the country. One suspects, however, that there has been no essential sacrifice of male authority in the structure of influence in the party or the government. In recent governments, for example, women have been assigned cabinet-level responsibilities uniquely in the French inspired Ministère des affaires sociales et de la promotion féminine. Although women have served in several sub-cabinet positions, notably in the ministries of justice and foreign affairs, women have not yet attained key positions of power and authority in Gabon. An examination of the publication *Les Elites gabonaises* supports the view that the overall progress of women into formal positions of influence remains modest. Of the approximately nine hundred persons designated as members of Gabon's elite in 1983, approximately thirty-six, or 4 percent, were women.[10] Although many Gabonese women clearly benefit from the egalitarian ideology that is implicit in Gabon's historical identification with France, traditional gender restrictions continue to limit the social mobility of many Gabonese women.

In a critical move, the party congress, at the request of the president, instituted a procedure for replacing the executive in case of death or disability. The position of vice president created during Mba's presidency and filled by Bongo was replaced in 1975 by the position of prime minister; in the new system adopted by the party congress, the president of the National Assembly will preside over a college composed of the prime minister, the minister of Defense, and an elected member of the party. It is the responsibility of this college to organize elections to fill the position of president.

Despite these moves that apparently increase intraparty democracy, party protocol exempts the president from direct criticism. In fact, Bongo has carefully developed an image as one who welcomes criticism—as long as it is leveled at others. Through the personality known as Makaya, criticism has evolved into a major asset for Bongo's presidency.

Makaya is an anonymous editorialist in the government-owned daily Libreville newspaper, *L'Union*. The column can be brutally critical of individual officials, the policies of ministries, or public or bureaucratic behavior; no one, with the notable exception of the president, is safe from Makaya's pen. Makaya is clearly the nom de plume of a number of persons, certainly including the president himself. Appearing to foster a climate of criticism that illustrates the sensitivity of the regime to the needs of the people, Makaya also enhances the power of the president by deliberately creating and sustaining the fear that anyone might be the next target. Makaya, as the French constitutional scholar François Hervouet observed, allows Bongo to serve as both government and opposition. Whatever the topic, the column receives wide attention, with much speculation about the identity of the author.[11] In 1986, Gabonese television adapted the Makaya concept to its own mode, creating the most controversial, and entertaining, program in its schedule. Twice weekly, ministerial figures appear on "Les dossiers de la télévision gabonais" (The files of Gabonese television) to answer questions, allegations, and accusations from a team of journalists from the state-operated media. To the apparent delight of viewers and, it is reported, President Bongo, invited ministers are frequently and pointedly called upon to explain and defend themselves. The programs often run several hours, providing an excellent opportunity for a skillful minister to build public and presidential confidence, while creating potentially disastrous situations for others; they provide Bongo with a dramatic opportunity to create another form of loyal opposition.[12]

There is little question that government control of the press extends beyond Makaya and surrogate forms of opposition such as "Les dossiers de la télévision gabonaise." The exercise of this power is graphically illustrated by the events that followed the publication of Pierre Péan's *Affaires africaines* in 1983. When publication of the book was announced in Paris, Bongo forbade all references to France in the government-owned media, including the quasi-public radio station, Africa Number 1. For five weeks France simply disappeared from media coverage, and French newspapers and newsmagazines were removed from circulation. This was the time of the attack on the U.S. Marines' compound in Beirut, with French, as well as U.S., military casualties. The incident received coverage in the Gabonese media, but without mention of the French role, providing an unusual, but vivid, example of the realities of power in Gabon.

Bongo's power and the stability of his regime depend on his adept control of the apparatus of the state, including the national police and the military forces. These sectors illustrate the complexities of power in contemporary Gabon. Both the military and the national police are controlled by a small group whose allegiance is to Bongo. Until 1987, the national police were commanded by Bongo's former brother-in-law, General Jean Boniface Assele. Assele apparently failed to maintain adequate intelligence about the activities of Bongo's estranged wife, Assele's sister Josephine, and he was replaced by a Bongo relative, Gaston Félicien Olouna.[13]

The military is linked to the Bongo government by a series of appointments that have assigned critical command positions to Bongo loyalists. Bongo himself is a trained pilot with a commission in the air force, and he maintains an important rapport with a corps of officers who have come of command age since 1970. In 1983, Bongo appointed three generals, Daniel Ba Oumar, André Nzong, and Assele, the key figures in the national defense structure, to positions on the Central Committee of the PDG, assuring continuity of control and elevating the status of the military and the national police in the hierarchy of influence. Bongo's apprehension about a coup is one obvious explanation for his careful attention to the role and status of the military in his regime. Some members of the junior officer class are apparently not content with the current state of affairs in the military. A corps of U.S.- and French-trained officers are reported to be dissatisfied with the lack of professionalism among the higher ranks of their services. Gabon's military is clearly top heavy, with at least 45 general rank officers in a combined army, navy, and air force of slightly more than 5,000 personnel. In such a close environment, frustration about advancement and reward would not be unexpected and may be exacerbated by the fact that critical command positions are not open to Gabonese officers. Some 125 French officers serve under contract to the government, and a contingent of French pilots has been assigned by the French Ministry of Defense to Gabon's small air force.

France's commitment to the stability of the regime is illustrated by the 500 marines at Camp de Gaulle near the Libreville airport. Mirage and Jaguar aircraft from the French air force are based on the military side of the Léon Mba airport, in easy view of visitors to the hotels and popular beaches in the vicinity. Although the terms of Gabon's military agreements with the French remain secret, there are periodic joint maneuvers, most recently in 1988, and the presence of French officers in the Gabonese military hierarchy assures an intimate French relationship with the Gabonese military. This relationship could prove troublesome to Bongo in the future; if a major challenge to the regime originated within the ranks of the Gabonese military, and the government in Paris decided not to intervene, an important foundation of Bongo's power would be weakened.

The Garde présidentielle (Presidential Guard) is responsible for the personal safety of the president, his family, and close associates. On permanent duty at the presidential palace in Libreville, the 1,500-member force is well trained and well equipped—and dominated by fellow Batékés whose loyalty to the president is considered unquestionable. The command and training of the guard is in the hands of French and Moroccan officers with a vested interest in maintaining the status quo. The longtime commander of the guard is a legendary veteran of Dien Bien Phu and Algeria, former Foreign Legionnaire, General "Loulou" Martin. In contrast with the conventional forces, the Garde présidentielle receives advanced military equipment; its remuneration and perquisites are superior to those received by personnel in the regular services. In effect, there are two military contingents in Gabon: a conventional force that fulfills traditional national defense functions, paralleled by a palace guard whose role is to maintain Bongo in power. If a contest arose between the two, the outcome of the confrontation might rest on a determination by the French on which side to support.[14]

THE POLITICAL PROCESS:
THE SEARCH FOR EQUILIBRIUM

During the Bongo era, politics in Gabon have been, to borrow a well-known phrase, a tangled web involving the French and Bongo family members and intimates in the use of the PDG and the apparatus of government to monopolize the process of decisionmaking. It is useful to envisage Gabonese politics during this era as the interplay of three critical elements seeking to maintain a state of political and economic equilibrium: First, the interests of the French weigh heavily in the national affairs of the country. From the standpoint of the government in Paris, Gabon is an important economic investment, and in the context of French foreign policy, a strategically placed ally in tropical Africa. For the 18,000 French who work and reside in Gabon, their economic well-being depends on the quality of Franco-Gabonese relations—or, to put the matter plainly, on Bongo's goodwill. The French population in Gabon is traditionally conservative, and conflicts between the Bongo regime and the expatriate French appear to be rare. In 1984, at the time of the Péan affair, the French community rallied to Bongo's support. Many longtime residents of Gabon feared expulsion in reprisal for the Mitterrand government's refusal to prohibit the publication of Péan's attack on Bongo. The size of the expatriate French population has, in fact, declined from an estimated 30,000 in the mid-1970s to its present size of approximately 18,000. This exodous reflects the volatility of the Gabonese economy in the 1980s and offers a warning to those who would too quickly characterize Bongo as a simple puppet of the French. Since independence, French influence has, at different times, both increased and waned, reflecting different ideologies of French regimes as well as shifts in Bongo's sense of the limits of Gabonese independence. Gabon's leadership was clearly apprehensive in 1981 following Mitterrand's first presidential victory, and Bongo was reported to be ecstatic about the prospects for a Chirac government in 1986. Due to mutual economic constraints and Gabon's growing nationalism, the cooperation accords between the countries have been renegotiated, leading to some reduction in the numbers of French nationals residing in Gabon. The decline in the demand for petroleum also took a toll among the resident French population, with a number of firms associated with the petroleum industry scaling back their activities. What is perhaps most significant is that Bongo has managed to establish an amicable relationship with each successive French regime since he assumed power in 1967. It appears that the French need Bongo as much as he needs them.

The second dynamic element of the political process is the Bongo family, comprising the followers and supporters of the president's relatives by blood and marriage; this group illustrates the extreme influence of family and ethnic ties in current Gabonese affairs. At the beginning of 1990, twelve of the forty-six cabinet positions were held by members of the president's ethnic group; members of his family have held key positions throughout the civilian and military bureaucracy. Bongo's estrangement from Josephine Assele led to a realignment of influence within "the family." Bongo's decision to substitute his nephew for the longtime head of the national police, Jean Boniface Assele, illustrated the seriousness of the division within this extended family. Assele's new position as minister of public works is decidedly less substantial than his previous post. There are indications, however, that Bongo's Assele sister-in-law continues to be an influential member of his inner circle.

The third dynamic force is composed of a varied group of presidential intimates, associates of Bongo's since his early years in the state bureaucracy. The oldest and most prominent members of this group are Léon Mébiame, Georges Rawiri, Louis Gaston Mayili, and Henri Minko; all four have held sensitive positions in the national government and have been key members of the Political Bureau of the PDG since its inception. In addition to this contingent of intimates, Bongo has made room for a number of Young Turks in both the party structure and the government. The leading members of this contingent are his son, the foreign minister, Ali Ben Bongo, and the former presidential chief of staff, Jean Ping, whose return from UNESCO in 1984 to Libreville was celebrated with the fanfare and ceremony usually reserved for a visiting head of state. Jean-Pierre Lemboumba-Lepandou, the minister of economic affairs, is another major influence within Bongo's inner circle.

Ethnicity plays a central role in this web of influence and personal relationships. Through his appointments and periodic reshuffling of ministerial positions, Bongo has attempted to maintain an ethnic balance throughout the system. Gabon's three largest ethnic groups, Fang, Bapounou, and Myéné, are historically well represented in the PDG and the civilian and military establishment. In the older contingent of intimates, the longtime prime minister, Mébiame, is an estuary Fang; the influential Rawiri, formerly ambassador to France and a Bongo associate since the

1960s, is from the Galoa (Myéné) community in Lambaréné; and Minko, who has held a wide variety of party and governmental positions, is commonly referred to as Bongo's man in the estuary Fang clans. Of Bongo's younger associates, Ping represents the Libreville Myéné community, and Lemboumba-Lepandou is from Franceville, the center of the Batéké population. As noted earlier, Bongo has carefully placed fellow Batékés in sensitive roles—a practice that may have sowed discord among some elements of the population. Bongo is not always well served by appointments of his relatives to important positions. In a widely publicized move in 1989, Bongo replaced his nephew, Martin Bongo, the minister of foreign affairs, with his son, Ali Ben Bongo. In a bitter attack on the *système Bongo*, Aristote Assam singled out Martin Bongo's lackluster performance as a prime example of governmental incompetence.[15]

Bongo orchestrates an intricate process of balancing interests and responding to an array of claims. At one moment, he is the champion of Gabonese national interests resisting the neocolonial practices of the French; on another occasion, he provides liberal investment conditions for foreign capital. When, for example, university students complained that their allowances were inadequate, Bongo negotiated directly with them. On several occasions, he has reversed ministerial decisions on educational policy. The essence of his approach is personal involvement and direct negotiations with any aggrieved party. Throughout this complex process, he has been assisted by Gabon's ample wealth allowing him to minimize the repercussions of dissent. Through firm control of the apparatus of state, including the military and security forces, and with the promise of French assistance in potentially dramatic circumstances, he has for nearly a quarter of a century maintained an intricate balance among Gabon's major interests.

In the process, Bongo and a number of his closest associates have amassed substantial fortunes. Bongo himself owns valuable properties in Gabon, France, and the United States, and he clearly enjoys the privileges of power. The new presidential palace in Libreville is built of Italian marble, and the presidential residences in Franceville and Port Gentil are equally imposing. But Bongo is, above all else, an astute politician with a shrewd sense of power. He remains autocratic, yet careful to nurture a broad base of popular support around the country. In a Gallup poll reported in 1986, 61.6 percent of the respondents indicated general satisfaction with the PDG and expressed their willingness to see an expansion of its powers. If the poll has any validity as a barometer of opinion about the president, it suggests that Bongo, after two decades in office, has managed to retain an important level of public support. In the presidential election of 1986—his third victory—Bongo received 99.6 percent of the votes. Running as usual in an uncontested election, Bongo campaigned

58

The presidential palace in Libreville (photo by the author).

Supporters of President Bongo and the PDG attending annual parade commemorating the founding of the PDG (photo by the author).

energetically in all the regions of the country seeking 100 percent endorsement.[16]

CHALLENGE AND CHANGE:
THE ROLE OF DISCONTENT

In spite of Bongo's success in retaining power for twenty-three years—or, more accurately, because of it—the accumulated weight of events in Gabon and abroad have initiated important pressures for change in the political system and raised fundamental questions about Bongo's future and Gabon's. Through the efficiency of a French-trained internal security system and zealous surveillance by many PDG members, there has been no systematic internal opposition to Bongo's regime. Occasional outbreaks of unrest have been quickly quelled, with participants in demonstrations against the regime imprisoned or exiled. It is apparent, however, that the accumulated effect of a number of these incidents, in conjunction with fundamental structural changes in eastern Europe and—perhaps more significant for Gabon—in Zaire and the Ivory Coast, have brought about a period of transition between the political style of the Bongo era and a pluralistic, possibly democratic, future that must be a surprise for even the most cynical observers of Gabonese politics. To further an understanding of the significance of these events, the following chronology is offered to illustrate the nature and character of the opposition to the Bongo regime:

1. In 1972, the government arrested and convicted a number of faculty at the national university for their alleged participation in the so-called Professor's Plot. The participants were accused of organizing Marxist-Leninist cells and of circulating subversive literature. In a curious twist of history, two major figures in the "plot," Pierre Agondo-Okawe and Joseph Rendjame, reappeared in 1990 as principals in the ranks of the opposition to Bongo.

2. In 1985, in a publicly televised execution, a young air force officer accused of plotting against the regime was shot by a firing squad at daybreak on a Libreville beach. The case is an interesting one. The officer, Captain Alexandre Mandja Ngokouta, reported to be a graduate of both French and U.S. military academies, was a member of a religious group, Christianisme céleste, whose members say they have been called to reform the morals of Gabonese society. Believing that he had received orders from God to assassinate Bongo, Ngokouta attempted to recruit fellow officers to his cause; he was reported by his confidants, tried, and executed.

3. Also in 1985, Aristote Assam, generally representing the views of the anti-Bongo expatriate community in Paris, produced a virulent attack on the *systéme Bongo*. Assam repeated Péan's assertion that Bongo was

personally responsible for a number of assassinations and mysterious deaths over the previous two decades, most notably that of Germain Mba. Assam charged Gabonese agents, in collusion with the French police and influential right-wing supporters, with harassing anti-Bongo partisans in France, and the Mitterrand regime with failure to support reform in Gabon. Assam's charges represented a systematic attempt to demonstrate that Bongo and influential members of his intimate circle, both French and Gabonese, have transformed Gabon into their private preserve, handsomely enriching themselves in the process.

4. In 1989, the Bongo regime experienced two attempted coups, neither very threatening, but putting the regime on notice that things were not well in Gabon. The first attempt, on September 23, appeared to be an effort by disgruntled Bapounou to seize power. According to the Gabonese minister of information, Zachary Myboto, a longtime Bongo ally, the key figure in the affair was Pierre Mamboundou, a Gabonese national employed in France by the Agence de coopération culturelle et technique. According to Myboto's official account, Mamboundou recruited several mercenaries in France who, upon their arrival in Gabon, were hidden by Mamboundou associates. What makes this event noteworthy is the closeness of several of the participants to President Bongo and the underlining of the continuing primacy of ethnic considerations in Gabonese politics. One of the conspirators, Lt. Colonel Georges Moubandjou, was formerly an aide-de-camp to Bongo, and a second conspirator, Valentin Nzambi, was a former minister and Bongo's adviser on issues involving Gabon's role in the international francophone community. From Paris and Dakar, Mamboundou denied any involvement in the plot, but acknowledged that he was, in fact, the leader of a previously unknown group, the Union du peuple gabonais. According to Myboto, the Gabonese conspirators were under observation by security personnel for some time prior to their arrest. The Mamboundou coup attempt took on added interest with Bongo's subsequent announcement that mercenaries of several European nationalities were involved. Bongo claimed that interests in Belgium, Luxembourg, and the Netherlands contributed mercenaries as an expression of discontent with France's special relationship with Gabon.[17]

The second coup attempt has comic book qualities. With information apparently uncovered in the investigation of the Mamboundou incident, Bongo announced on November 24 that Abdoulaye Diallo, a supposed Malian drug dealer also described in official releases as the leader of a religious sect, Koulouhoum, and several accomplices had been arrested for planning a coup d'état. The most serious dimension of the plot was in its aftermath: two persons detained in the incident died in police custody. A French national, Richard Anton, a former employee of the defunct Bank of Luxembourg and Gabon, was reported to have died of an acute case of malaria; and a Gabonese national, Doukakis Nziengui, an employee of the nationalized energy and water department, the Société d'énergie et eaux du Gabon (SEEG), died of an apparent heart attack at a Libreville hospital.

These events substantiate the existence of long-standing expressions of discontent in Gabon. The Professor's Plot and Assam's book illustrated the evolution of the Gabonese Fang to a situation of uneasy plurality; Alexandre Ngokouta's execution and the arrest of the Malian guru, Diallo point to the regime's obsession with hostile, alien influences in the country (Ngokouta's organization, Christianisme céleste was reported to have originated in Benin, and several members of the Bongo government, including one of the accused plotters, were said to have been under the subversive influence of Koulohoum). In fact, the Bongo government has perfected the art of scapegoating non-Gabonese residents for the ills and woes of the country. In a display of official xenophobia in 1986, Bongo blamed non-Gabonese African expatriates for prostitution and drug addiction in Gabon.

In contrast to these apparently unrelated events, systematic and sustained opposition to the Bongo regime was mounted by the Mouvement de redressement national (MORENA), until 1989 a Fang-led exile group in Paris. MORENA appears to have originated in 1981 at the time of the distribution of the anonymously authored "White Paper" criticizing the Bongo regime and proposing a return to multipartyism and parliamentary democracy. Suspicion was that the paper was prompted by Aubame's return to Gabon and represented an attempt by dissident Fang to create an underground opposition. Several disturbances took place on the campus of the national university in Libreville, and a number of faculty and students, including the rector of the university, were arrested. When the arrest of the rector, Jean-Pierre Nzoghe-Nguema, sparked additional unrest, the Bongo government confronted its first real internal crisis. In an effort to eliminate MORENA, the government arrested, imprisoned, or exiled a number of persons, including Samuel Mba, editor of the government newspaper, L'Union, and a prominent member of Léon Mba's cabinet, and Jean-Marc Ekoh, who had earlier been convicted for joining Aubame's provisional government following the short-lived coup d'état of 1964. Mba, Ekoh, and others arrested were Fang, heightening suspicion that the incident had provided Bongo with an excellent opportunity to eliminate his rivals, real or imagined. Ekoh's fall was particularly noteworthy, as he was by all accounts a brilliant intellectual with an unlimited future in Gabonese public life.

Following these events in Libreville, MORENA mounted a campaign in Paris to convince the French government to take action against the Bongo regime. Hopes raised by Mitterrand's election in May 1981 were increased by Amnesty International's 1984 report on the 1982 conspiracy trial.[18] Amnesty's observer at the trial reported a number of procedural irregularities, most notably that the defendants were denied legal assistance during their pretrial detainment and that lawyers representing the defendants were given no opportunity to interrogate prosecution witnesses. In Amnesty's view, these procedural irregularities alone constituted a miscarriage of justice. Even more serious were the charges of brutality and torture. Amnesty noted reports extending over a decade's time that prisoners were systematically beaten and tortured in Gabonese prisons by personnel from Gabon's internal security organization, the Centre de documentation (CEDOC). Brutal treatment by the intelligence unit of the national police was also reported, with torture by water immersion, electric shock, and tobacco poisoning (induced by forcing prisoners to consume large amounts of tobacco in a very short period); these were techniques the French were alleged to have employed extensively during the Algerian conflict. Amnesty pointedly noted that the Gabonese security forces have traditionally been headed by former members of French security organizations. In fact, CEDOC was under the direction of a French officer, Colonel Conan for many years, until his resignation in 1989 for personal reasons. Finally, former prisoners complained of being forced to wear arm and leg irons for long periods without medical attention.

Amnesty's report concluded that the charges against the defendants were essentially without foundation and that their treatment violated the international standards contained in Article 33 of the UN Agreement on the Treatment of Prisoners. Allegations of torture and brutality in Gabon's central prison in Libreville were repeated in the 1989 report by the U.S. Department of State on human rights in Gabon.[19]

In 1986, in response to Bongo's renewed call for national reconciliation, two leading MORENA figures, the former spokesman of the organization, André Nbaobame, and the former secretary-general, Parfait Anotho Edowisa, returned to Gabon and were elected to the Central Committee of the PDG. Edowisa was a leader in a radical wing of MORENA with ties to several influential members of the French Socialist party. Edowisa's decision to return to Gabon illustrated both the frustration of exile and Bongo's willingness to risk the presence of potential opponents in the country. It now appears that these decisions were the prelude to a series of events that continue to unfold. Following Edowisa's return to Gabon, MORENA's new secretary-general, Max Anicet Koumba-Mbadinga, formed a Gabonese government in exile and appealed to the French government for recognition as the legitimate government of Gabon. Predictably, the French proved reluctant. In a series of events culminating in Prime Minister Pierre Mauroy's conciliatory words in Libreville in 1984 following the Péan affair, the Mitterrand government made peace with the Bongo government, responding more directly to French strategic needs in Gabon than to MORENA's claims of oppression.

MORENA began as an alliance of three organizations: the more radical Socialist wing previously led by Edowisa; a student organization, the Association des étudiants gabonais, led by André Obame Mba; and the Parti national gabonais, whose most prominent member is Paul Mba Abessole, a Catholic priest with important links to the Fang population in the Woleu N'Tem province. In what may be the most important move of his presidency, Bongo entered into a dialogue with Abessole in May 1989 that culminated in the priest's return to Gabon in fall 1989 after thirteen years of exile.

Abessole's heralded return to Gabon produced results that neither he nor Bongo could have possibly predicted. Bongo's motive in securing Abessole's return was probably a continuation of his traditionally successful policy of convincing outspoken opponents of his regime to return to Gabon—a practice that began with Germain Mba in 1968, and included, most recently, Abessole's fellow exiles in Paris, Nbaobame and Edowisa. Abessole's reasons for leaving Paris no doubt included the usual frustration of exile and the hope that on the scene he could accomplish more than by repeated futile attempts to convince the French government to discipline Bongo, let alone recognize MORENA's government in exile as the legitimate government of Gabon. Whatever the causes, the result of Abessole's return to Gabon in May 1989 was the inauguration of a process of change and liberalization that may require decades to complete.

Abessole's arrival occurred at a time of unrest. Prolonged and intensely unpopular measures of economic austerity prompted by the recession of 1986–1987, an atmosphere of anxiety created by the attempted coups of 1989, and the apparent end of one-party monopolies in Zaire and the Ivory Coast produced a climate of anticipation and tension. It might be said that winds of change had reached Libreville, but growing discontent about the government's economic policies provided the underlying basis for the tension. Disturbances broke out in Libreville and Port Gentil in January 1990 following the government's announcement that it intended to continue its austerity program. In the first serious display of discontent since 1982, unusually large numbers of people engaged in street demonstrations and attacked government buildings. In this climate of growing frustration and discontent, Bongo moved skillfully to accommodate the pressures for change. He announced a "Conference on Democracy" to discuss the future of the Gabonese political system. The announcement of the conference explicitly rejected any form of multipartyism, and after several delays, the conference convened on March 27, 1990, attended by MORENA representatives and a range of persons representing various organizations and interests within the "corporate state." In an effort to maintain control, Bongo assigned his longtime associate, First Deputy Prime Minister Georges Rawiri as the conference organizer. The presiding officer of the conference was an Abessole coreligionist and fellow northern Fang, Monsignor Basile Mve, the bishop of Oyem. Bongo's son and minister of foreign affairs, Ali Ben Bongo, and Jean Ping, the presidential chief of staff, were, in addition to Rawiri, the president's men at the conference. In what appears to be a classic case of unanticipated results, the conference report concluded, "A monolithic system is incompatible with the present evolution of Gabonese society" and, in a phrase quite uncharacteristic for Gabon, asserted, "Democracy, universally understood, has a pluralistic character."[20]

With specific reference to President Bongo and his role in this democratic future, the conference participants agreed to "respect the presidential mandate" as long as Bongo expressed willingness to "remain above the parties."[21] The presidential term of office was reduced from seven years to five and limited to one term, in effect restricting Bongo's presidency to no more than eight additional years (that is, until the conclusion of his present term in 1993, plus a five-year term that would conclude in 1998). In reality, what appears to have emerged from the conference is a presidential system intriguingly similar to the model that has evolved in France under Mitterrand. One can expect that Bongo will, following the Mitterrand style, concentrate on policy questions involving foreign and economic affairs and leave the day-to-day business of government in the hands of the prime minister. In fact, a Gabonese version of the French relationship between the president and prime minister could be an ideal arrangement for President Bongo.

It is likely that serious divisions within the opposition as well as the residual power of the incumbent president limited the actions of the representatives to the conference. MORENA has now divided into two wings—the former, and aging, Paris exiles led by Abessole now known as the *bûcherons* (woodcutters) and more militant young Gabonese Fang increasingly restless with the Bongo regime. Observers noted the emergence of seventy-four different expressions of opinion at the conference—a phenomenon no doubt related to the relaxation of previous limits on discourse and, as in the aftermath of *glasnost* in the Soviet Union, the rapid and potentially destabilizing appearance of long-suppressed ethnic considerations, accumulated grievances, and personal ambitions.[22] Following the conference, with its important affirmation of pluralistic democracy, Bongo took several critical steps that may have been designed to ward off further reductions in his power or even his removal from office. In a dramatic move reminiscent of his decision in 1968 to dissolve the political parties of that era, Bongo proposed the dissolution of the PDG and its replacement, following a celebrated Gaullist precedent, with a new all-Gabonese unity organization, the Rassemblement social-démocrate gabonais (RSDG); the distinction between *rassemblement* (rally) and "political party" borrows from de Gaulle's creation of the Rassemblement du peuple français (RPF) immediately after World War II in an attempt to build a political constituency that transcended the traditional ideological divisions of French politics.

Within weeks of this move, Bongo struck again, removing the incumbent prime minister, Léon Mébiame, and naming a virtual outsider, Casimir Oyé Mba, then the director of the Central African development bank, Banque des états de l'Afrique centrale (BEAC), as his replacement. Mba's appointment signaled Bongo's determination to maintain the stability of the regime by choosing a fresh face—but one with demonstrated ethnopolitical credentials. Mba, an estuary Fang, could bring Bongo some relief from criticisms that Mébiame, also a Fang from the estuary and longtime Bongo associate, was simply a figurehead. Mba's technocratic credentials and prestige minimized the predictable criticism that he was only a stalking horse for Bongo. It is possible, as several observers have suggested, that Sese Seko Mobutu's precedent of choosing an unknown as head of government during Zaire's period of transition was a factor in Bongo's decision.

Bongo's apparently successful efforts to steer events toward a peaceful conclusion were dramatically interrupted by serious violence in Libreville and Port Gentil on May 24, 1990. These events appear to have been precipitated by the death of a Bongo opponent, Joseph Rendjame, a prominent member of one of the newly formed opposition groups, the Parti du progrés gabonais (PPG). Reports of Rendjame's death by poisoning in a Libreville hotel provoked riots in Libreville and Port Gentil. The government dispatched troops to Port Gentil at the same time as the French decided to supplement their military contingent with a company of Foreign Legionnaires from Corsica to protect French nationals, particularly in Port Gentil, where the most serious rioting appears to have taken place. The French intervention evoked memories of 1964, although French officials, including President Mitterrand, proclaimed French neutrality throughout the crisis. Personnel of the major French-Gabonese petroleum company, Elf Gabon, were evacuated for several days, leading Bongo to declare that he would replace the company if it did not immediately resume work. Although calm was restored within a few days, and Elf Gabon resumed production of petroleum, the incident evidenced serious discontent and tension in the country. The events of May 24 are both ironic and unfortunate in that they followed so closely on Bongo's May 21 announcement ending the one-party era with an amendment to the constitution that prepared the return to multipartyism. With these critical moves, Bongo accomplished two significant objectives: appearing to provide an embryonic foundation for a post-Bongo era while, at least for the moment, preserving his position in the face of an important challenge to his power. In all likelihood, Bongo simply bowed to the inevitable without real enthusiasm for the changes that he ushered in during the first critical six months of 1990.

On the heels of the disturbances in Port Gentil and Libreville, in consultation with opposition leaders, Bongo revised the election schedule that had been agreed upon during the March Democracy conference; at that time, there had been tentative agreement on holding elections for a reconstituted National Assembly in October 1990. Possibly frightened by the prospect of further disturbances and the specter of losing power completely, the government announced that two rounds of legislative elections would take place on September 23 and 30—a month earlier than planned. In accord with Bongo's accomplished art of cooptation, each opposition organization received an initial allocation of F CFA 20 million (approximately U.S.$50,000). Following the initial round, each party that won at least one seat in the legislature received an additional allocation of F CFA 30 million (U.S.$75,000), and a jeep.[23]

The elections took place in a climate of anticipation and some apprehension; Prime Minister Casimir Oyé Mba countered charges that the government "stuffed" ballot boxes with accusations of opposition intimidation and harassment. For all the fanfare, the results were initially inconclusive: 58 persons were selected in the two rounds of balloting, but results in 32 voting districts were annulled. Prime Minister Mba's decision to annul these results was based on reports of widespread fraud and intimidation of voters by the opposition. Replacement elections for the remaining 62 seats were immediately rescheduled for the following month, according to the original schedule agreed upon in March.

The appearance of groups and leaders together with the precipitous decline in the credibility of the Bongo regime during the prolonged period of economic austerity resulted in a direct challenge to Bongo's claim of widespread public support. Bongo's proposed replacement for the PDG, the hastily contrived Rassemblement social-démocrate gabonais, vanished immediately as both the government and the opposition groups adhered to their separate agendas. The political environment was not, however, conducive to opponents' efforts to fully demonstrate their political strength. Gabon's complex ethnic patterns limited unambiguous anti-Bongo alliances among the opposition candidates, and the decision to hold elections on relatively short notice gave the PDG an appreciable advantage in a number of jurisdictions.

The PDG was the victor in both the September elections and the replacement elections during the last two weeks of October; PDG candidates won 44 of the 58 seats contested in the two rounds of elections in September, and gained an additional 18 seats in the October elections. In the reconstituted National Assembly (following agreement at the Democracy conference to increase the size of the legislature to 120 members), the PDG became the governing party upon winning 62 of the 120 seats contested in the election. Although it holds a narrow two-seat majority, the PDG received pledges of support from several small opposition groups that should allow it to control the legislature. The real story of the elections, however—and a critical element in the PDG victory—lies in the controversial decision of the major opposition figure, Paul Mba Abessole, the MORENA-Bûcheron leader, to boycott the replacement elections of October. Events in Gabon were becoming curiouser and curiouser.

On Sunday, October 21, the first day of the resheduled elections, Abessole issued a communiqué in the name of MORENA calling for a boycott of the elections. This directive to his followers expressed disappointment and anger at the government's decision to annul the September results in a number of constituencies. Abessole was also the only opposition leader not elected to the legislature in the first round of elections in September, and in his eyes and those of many of his supporters, his defeat was the result of fraudulent government practices. Abessole's failure to receive a seat in the National Assembly was a serious setback to his aspirations to the prime ministership and, eventually, perhaps the presidency. Although it is quite likely that the government interfered in the electoral process, some speculated that Abessole had moved dangerously close to Bongo and that his long period of exile had distanced him from a younger, more militant Fang constituency. Whatever Abessole's motives, his decision certainly removed an important obstacle to a PDG victory and reinforced Casimir Oyé Mba's political standing as a major contender for leadership in the post-Bongo era. Throughout this remarkable period, President Bongo, following his earlier promise, played the role of statesman staying above the fray.[24]

The outcome of the replacement elections in October confirmed the pattern of the September elections, with support for PDG candidates largely confined to the president's Haut-Ogooué province and the adjacent Ogooué-Ivindo and Ogooué-Lolo provinces. MORENA-Bûcheron candidates elected in the first round of elections in September were successful in the Fang areas of central and northern Gabon and in the large Fang community in the estuary. Although their fortunes were no doubt affected by Abessole's decision to withdraw from participation following the September elections, MORENA-Bûcheron candidates won 15 seats in the

National Assembly, with one seat going to the MORENA fundamentalists. After MORENA-Bûcheron, the other major victor in the election was the Parti gabonais du progrés (PGP). Candidates of the PGP ran well in the Myéné communities in Lambaréné and Port Gentil and elected 6 members to the National Assembly. Interest in the PGP was heightened by the controversial circumstances of Joseph Rendjame's death in Libreville at the time of the Democracy conference, and the prominence of a number of PGP candidates in the predominantly Myéné constituencies of Lambaréné and Port Gentil. The leader of the PGP, Pierre Agondo-Okawe, is a well-known figure in Gabonese politics. He was one of those accused in the Professor's Plot in 1972 along with Joseph Rendjame and served, as well, as the lawyer who represented Germain Mba's family following his controversial death in 1971.

The combined performance of PGP and MORENA-Bûcheron candidates represents a significant political statement and creates the stage for an extended drama involving Bongo, the PDG, and the new participants. Despite Paul Mba Abessole's ambivalence, the elections appear to be a decisive mandate by the Gabonese for political and economic reform and, significantly, a strong expression of support for organizations like MORENA with close ties to the Catholic church. Abessole's role, although possibly diminished, and that of Bishop Mve at the March conference point strongly to a renewal of Catholic influence in Gabonese affairs.

It would be unfortunate if these very serious events are not interpreted correctly. The 1964 coup d'état still stands as the single most important event in postindependence Gabon. One should not forget that it represented widespread dissatisfaction with Mba's regime. As Joachim Pallard's report pointed out, the unrest was not limited to the small cadre of officers who implemented the coup, but involved widespread frustration and discontent about the direction of the country and the attitudes and behavior of those who governed. Pallard mentioned problems of corruption and favoritism and the corrosive effects of power. According to Aristote Assam, the partisans of MORENA, and a varied group of critics, the Bongo regime is susceptible to the same charges that motivated the attempt to overthrow Léon Mba. A report on May 25, 1990, in the Paris newspaper *Libération* charged that a number of Gabonese had engaged in the transfer of billions of French francs annually to Swiss and French banks. In the face of such direct allegations and mounting internal opposition, the events of spring and fall 1990 are a clear sign that a day of reckoning approaches. Gabon's immediate future depends on the ability of its leaders to learn—or relearn—the rudiments of democratic politics. At the same time, Gabon's intimate ties with France, reflecting its traditional tutelage and dependence, may create a unique opportunity for a true developmental partnership.

NOTES

1. Mba's views are cited by François Hervouet, "Le processus de concentration des pouvoirs par le président de la république au Gabon," *Penant: Revue de droit des pays d'Afrique*, no. 779 (January–March 1983), p. 12.

2. Mba's account of the events was reported in *L'agence gabonaise d'information: Bulletin quotidien*, no. 41 (February 20, 1964), pp. 1–3.

3. For different perspectives on the February coup, see "Gabon: Putsch or Coup d'Etat, *Africa Report*, vol. 9, no. 3 (March 1964), pp. 12–15; and Charles B. Darlington and Alice F. Darlington, *African Betrayal* (New York: David McKay, 1968), Chapters 1–3.

4. There is a full discussion of the international legal dimensions of the French intervention in Gabon in Sung Ho Kim, "Intervention at the Request of Incumbent Governments," Ph.D. diss., Columbia University, 1974, pp. 145–187.

5. Captain Joachim Pallard, "Evénements des 18, 19, et 20 Fevrier, 1964," memorandum to President Mba, February 20, 1964 (translated by the author). The author found Pallard's report to Mba in a carton of uncatalogued material in the Gabon National Archives. That it was included in a collection of material that came from the president's office suggests that it did come to the attention of President Mba.

6. See Hervouet, "Le processus de concentration des pouvoirs par le président de la république au Gabon," pp. 18–20.

7. Pierre Péan, *Affaires africaines* (Paris: Fayard, 1983), pp. 128–166.

8. For discussions of the Bongo era and the evolution of the PDG, see Oliver Duhamel, "Le parti démocratique gabonais," *Revue française d'études politiques africaines*, no. 125 (May 1976), pp. 24–27; Gilbert Comte, "La république gabonaise: Treize années d'histoire," *Revue française d'études politiques africaines*, 90 (June 1973), pp. 39–57; Pierre Vermeil, "Le parti démocratique gabonais," *Le mois en Afrique*, no. 176–177 (August–September 1980), pp. 9–10; François Gaulme, *Le Gabon et son ombre* (Paris: Editions Karthala, 1988), pp. 130–161; and Marc de Saint-Paul Aicardi, *Gabon: The Development of a Nation* (London: Routledge, 1989), pp. 23–37. Aicardi's book was published initially in French as *Le Gabon: du roi Denis à Omar Bongo* (Paris: Albatros, 1987).

9. Laurent Essone-Ndong, "Les syndicats du Gabon," *Annales de l'école nationale d'administration* (Libreville), 1 (1977), pp. 47–53.

10. *Les Elites gabonaises*, 2nd ed. (Paris: Ediafric la documentation africaine, 1983).

11. Hervouet, "Le processus de concentration des pouvoirs par le président de la république au Gabon," pp. 30–32.

12. Lawrence Greisheimer, "Ministers get their TV come-uppance in Gabon," *Manchester Guardian Weekly*, January 5, 1986, p. 12.

13. For a description of Bongo's security apparatus, see "Gabon: Bongo's Security," *Africa Confidential*, 26, no. 22 (October 30, 1985), pp. 6–7.

14. Péan, *Affaires africaines*, pp. 150–154; Economist Intelligence Unit (EIU), Country Profile, *Gabon, 1989–90*, p. 5.

15. Aristote Assam, *Omar Bongo, ou la racine du mal gabonais* (Paris: Pensée Universelle, 1985), p. 29.

16. For an excellent analysis of the Bongo era, see Michael C. Reed, "Gabon: A Neo-Colonial Enclave of Enduring French Interests," *Journal of Modern African Studies*, 25, no. 2 (1987), pp. 283–320.

17. This information is compiled from EIU Country Reports, *Congo, Gabon, Equatorial Guinea*, nos. 1–4, 1989–1990.

18. Amnesty International, *Gabon: Déni de justice au cours d'un procés* (London: Amnesty International Publications, 1984); for Amnesty's conclusions on the trial see pp. 17–21.

19. *U.S. Department of State Country Reports on Human Rights Practices for 1989* (Washington, D.C.: Government Printing Office, 1989), p. 124.

20. A partial text of the conference was reported in *Jeune Afrique* (April 23, 1990), pp. 6–7 (translation by the author).

21. *Ibid.*, p. 7.

22. Francis Kpatindé, "Portrait: Paul Mba Abessole—les parcours sinuex d'un opposant dans l'âme," *Jeune Afrique*, no. 1563 (December 12–18, 1990), pp. 28–29.

23. Francis Kpatindé, "Le Gabon entre Bongo et les Bûcherons," *Jeune Afrique*, no. 1558 (November 7–13, 1990), pp. 28–29.

24. *Ibid.*, p. 28.

3

The Economy

Gabon's transition from colony to nation-state barely disturbed the pattern of economic relationships with France. At the time of independence in 1960, the French concluded a number of agreements with the Gabonese that guaranteed a continuing, preeminent role for the French in Gabonese economic affairs. These agreements appeared to illustrate France's willingness to transform the former colonial relationship into a commitment to assist the new Gabonese state along the difficult, precarious path of development. In fact, they built on the pre-existing framework for Gabonese dependency on the French. Michel Debré, de Gaulle's prime minister at the time, stated explicitly that *coopération* was the quid pro quo for independence.[1] In later years, the French often cited Sékou Touré's decision to take Guinea on its own solitary journey, and the subsequent problems the Guineans encountered, as the fate of those who refused the French hand stretched out to them. Mba and Aubame initially accepted the idea of Gabonese participation in the proposed French Community for precisely that reason: It was apparent to the Gabonese leadership that economic development would be extraordinarily difficult, perhaps impossible, without French assistance.

THE FRENCH ROLE IN THE ECONOMY

Gabon's incorporation into the new equatorial federation in 1910 established both its modern economic orientation and the continuing structure of French control over the economy. During the AEF era, administrative control of Gabonese economic and political affairs was vested in the governor-general in Brazzaville, relegating Gabon to second-class citizenship. Gabon received unfavorable tax and tariff considerations, even though its timber industry contributed disproportionately to the AEF treasury. After World War II, Gabonese leaders routinely criticized the AEF administration for its lack of support and, more to the point, for its refusal to adopt a policy of economic diversification, but Brazzaville remained content to collect taxes on the substantial profits from Gabonese timber and do little to assist the Gabonese in the development of a critically needed transportation network. At the time of independence, Gabon's road system was one of the least developed in the AEF territory. Although terrain and climate produced staggering problems of construction and maintenance, the unequal distribution of resources within the federation was a major reason for the poor condition of the roads. Port facilities, particularly at Port Gentil, were accelerated, however, in conjunction with the development of *okoumé* and, later, petroleum, as important export commodities. Overall, Gabon's economy developed in direct proportion to French interest in its natural resources, producing an economy that relied until the 1970s almost exclusively on France for capital investment and markets for its export commodities. During the colonial era, the French reinforced their economic supremacy with a legal code implementing French colonialism. French policy emphasized private enterprise, as Pierre Claver Maganga-Moussavou explained in his study of Gabonese dependence on France:

> The purpose of all these measures relating to French capital was not only to assure a good rate of return and favorable amortization conditions, but also to assure relatively low production costs since French colonial products had to be competitive if they were to survive on the international market.[2]

Gabon's current investment code embodies the same principles. Gabon's two presidents, Mba and Bongo, have maintained Gabon's commitment to free enterprise with an enduring hostility toward collective solutions, either in the name of African or European socialism. In fact, free enterprise in Gabon is partially fiction. Effectively, the government protects a group of monopolies that dominate the Gabonese economic scene. Even in the competitive petroleum game, the government grants licenses for exploration through a complex bidding process. A more accurate description of the Gabonese economy would be that it combines elements of state capitalism and limited private enterprise. State involvement reflects an interest in controlling the scope and pace of economic development, but also provides the leading figures of the regime with direct economic benefits. Foreign firms are expected to offer participation in their affairs to the key figures of the regime, and direct financial involvement in an array of enterprises sanctioned by the state provides a source of considerable wealth for strategically placed members of Gabon's elite.

At an institutional level, the pervasive role of the French in the Gabonese economy appears in the French participation in all major sectors of the economy. The French national oil company, Elf Aquitaine, holds 60 percent of the stock of its Gabonese subsidiary, Elf Gabon, which controls nearly 70 percent of Gabonese petroleum production. French and U.S. interests control approximately 60 percent of the stock of the Compagnie minière de l'Ogooué (COMILOG), the manganese holding company, with the Gabonese government holding 30 percent. French interests together constitute more than 60 percent of the shares of the Compagnie des mines de Franceville (COMUF), the uranium consortium, and receive 70 percent of the total production; the Gabonese government controls 25 percent of the shares.[3] In the most traditional sector of the economy, the timber industry, French interests have been the predominant force since the late nineteenth century.

In 1972, in an effort to increase revenues and secure an enhanced national role in the affairs of the major French firms, the Bongo government successfully renegotiated the 1960 accords establishing the initial division of ownership between French interests and the newly independent Gabonese government. The most notable feature of the new agreements was a 10 percent surtax on the gross profits of all foreign firms in Gabon. In 1977, the government called for more favorable terms for Gabonese participation in all the major sectors of the economy; its avowed goal was to acquire at least 49 percent participation in all firms doing business in the country. Although the government has not yet obtained this level of ownership, the effort illustrates the increasing complexities in economic interactions between the French and the Gabonese. Although independence did not bestow complete autonomy upon the Gabonese, it did provide the government with an important degree of leverage in dealing with the French. Gabon remains a client state of France's but independence did create the form, if not the complete substance, of national sovereignty. Although the Gabonese demand for a surtax in 1972 angered the French, they were obliged to respect the right of a sovereign state to make such decisions involving its fundamental national interests. Economically, Gabon's leverage in its dealings with France reflects the value of its exports, primarily petroleum, in the international markets, and the corresponding relative freedom from France created by this independent income. Gabonese dependency on France is, nevertheless, extensive. Gabon is a member of the African "franc zone," whose unit of currency, the CFA franc, is set in value in relation to the French franc at a ratio of 50 to 1.[4] French and, more recently, U.S. capital and technology play an integral role in the production of Gabon's principal export products, and efforts to diversify the economy have produced new tensions as well as new participants; since 1970, the World Bank and the International Monetary Fund (IMF) have become intimately involved in Gabonese economic development.

In the private sector, as Maganga-Moussavou found, there are no truly Gabonese firms. The private firms that do exist are affiliates of foreign, primarily French businesses. Nor is there a truly Gabonese entrepreneurial class. With the exception of some examples of *petit commerce*, economic activity is principally the function of the state or foreign interests. Although Gabon's 1987 agreements with the IMF to promote private enterprise might provide an opening for Gabonese entrepreneurs, unless the government restricts participation to Gabonese nationals, this opportunity will likely be filled by expatriates who already control many retail and wholesale activities throughout the country. Libreville and Port Gentil, for example, offer virtually endless illustrations of expatriate involvement in the service sector. Such basic services as insurance, automobile repair, and pharmacies are owned and operated by third- and fourth-generation French residents. In recent years, the French expatriate community—currently estimated at 18,000—and historically one of the largest in the former French colonies, has been joined by Senegalese, Lebanese, and Syrian merchants, who have added a distinctly new dimension to the world of Gabonese business affairs. In the face of expatriate monopolies, many Gabonese have sought economic security in the ranks of Gabon's large civil service.

France is also the primary source of external financial assistance for Gabon, primarily through two channels: the Fonds d'aide et de coopération (FAC) and the more commercially oriented Caisse centrale de coopération économique (CCCE). The role of the FAC in Gabon is instructive. Assistance from this agency of the French Ministry of Cooperation covers mines, industry, and energy; social and sanitary facilities; teaching and teacher preparation; and cultural activities and information. Between 1959 and 1979, FAC allocated more than U.S.$1 billion to Gabon, approximately 60 percent for the development of infrastructure, including such priorities as the Transgabonais railway and improvement of the port at Owendo. These funds evidence the overriding interest of the French government in creating an attractive environment for continuing French investment and the maintenance of France's institutional role in the Gabonese economy.

The second channel for French funds and influence into the economy is the CCCE. In addition to disbursing FAC funds,the CCCE acts as a conduit for funds from the French Ministry of Economics to the Gabonese government, the Gabonese Development Bank, and other state enterprises responsible for investment and economic development. Since 1960, funds from the CCCE have gone into hydroelectric facilities, the cement factory at Owendo, telecommunications projects, and Air Gabon. CCCE expenditures emphasize infrastructure and the development of a professional cadre of personnel in such state-operated enterprises as water, electricity, and gas.[5]

It is difficult to assess the relationship between the FAC and the CCCE; there is clearly some duplication of effort and the priorities of the two agencies are not necessarily identical. The CCCE continues a funding system begun during World War II by de Gaulle's government in exile in London and represents the long-standing interest of the French government in the former colonies. The lineage of the FAC is equally revealing: At the time of independence, the Ministry of the Colonies was replaced by the Ministry of Cooperation, a change designed to reflect the new relationship between the former colonies and the metropole. In this transition, FAC funding replaced the Fonds d'investissements pour le développement économique et social (FIDES), the government investment fund used throughout the former French colonies to develop economic activities of value to the French. It was not readily apparent at the time that the change in title represented a fundamental shift in French priorities in their economic or political relationships with their former colonies; France's abrupt and rapid withdrawal from Guinea after its declaration of independence stands out as a reminder of French intentions. Postindependence FAC funding maintains the historical emphasis on creating favorable conditions and returns for French investment.

The combined contributions of these two French agencies to Gabon is substantial. From 1982 to 1987, French assistance to Gabon totaled the equivalent of U.S.$339 million, an average of approximately U.S.$56 million per year. During the same period, assistance from all other sources amounted to approximately U.S.$83 million. In 1989, Gabon received the highest percentage—16 percent—of French aid distributed to francophone sub-Saharan Africa. The net result is a persistent French influence on the scope and direction of Gabonese economic development and a continuation of direct economic benefits to the French government and private investors.[6]

THE MAJOR REVENUE PRODUCERS: TIMBER AND PETROLEUM

The transition from luxury products like gold and ivory to such primary resources as rubber and timber reflects the revolution in industrial technology that took place in the nineteenth and twentieth centuries. Gabon was able to weather the storm of transition because the French needed these resources for their own economic development. Investment in timber, for example, quadrupled between 1875 and 1925, creating the industry that remained the backbone of the Gabonese economy until the late 1950s.

An aerial photograph of Gabon's logging regions would show an intricate network of access routes developed over the years to transport

Logging *okoumé* in the Lake region near Lambaréné, circa 1925 (photo courtesy of the Gabon National Archives).

logs to the coast for finishing and shipping. The Ogooué River, easily navigable from Ndjolé in the near interior to Port Gentil on the coast south of Libreville, together with its major tributaries plays an indispensable role in transporting logs from the interior to the coast. *Okoumé* is a soft, reddish, lightweight wood that is perfectly suited to transportation by water. Heavier woods, such as *azobi* and *miama*, are moved by the fleets of logging trucks that are a familiar and often dangerous presence on Gabon's limited road system. The logging industry is severly hindered by Gabon's two rainy seasons, during which many of the unpaved roads are impassable.

In 1955, the colonial administration restricted the harvesting areas and instituted the first serious conservation measures. This was the first significant limitation on the logging industry since the initial regulatory measure of creating logging zones in 1931. Although exports of *okoumé* declined during the war years, postwar construction demands for Gabonese wood products led to a rapid increase in production and depletion of the supply of exportable woods in the accessible coastal areas. Three zones presently represent the total supply of timber for local use and the export market. The first zone is reserved for Gabonese, reflecting a concern for the rural population. The lower Ogooué, Fernan Vaz, and estuary regions are the primary targets of the government's effort to sustain a source of income in areas where alternative economic activities are prohibited by the dense forest cover. Until the 1970s, this diverse area accounted for nearly 20 percent of the timber produced in the country. The zone has, however, experienced a marked decline in production following many years of intense harvesting and inadequate reforestation. For a number of years, most recently in 1988, the CCCE has funded reforestation in the estuary region south of Libreville in an effort to revitalize the local timber economy.

The commercial zone, that is, the zone of major corporate exploitation, is a vast area comprising the south-central region including N'Gounié, the area between Ndjolé and Fougamou, the Cristal Mountains in the northeast, and the southern coastal region around Mayomba. Nearly twenty firms are involved in harvesting timber in this zone, which provides the major supply of *okoumé* for both the export and domestic markets.

The third zone is a remote area in the eastern part of the country that is dependent on the completion of the Transgabonais railway for its development. In 1971, the government granted concessions to a number of major firms to remove timber from this area, but no substantial harvesting has yet taken place. Estimates are that timber production in this region could more than double the supply for the export market, but the area remains virtually inaccessible and production is now additionally constrained by the general economic depression affecting the demand for Gabonese wood products.

Since 1975, the Société nationale des bois de Gabon (SNBG) has controlled the pricing and marketing of Gabon's timber. Prior to that time, Gabon and the neighboring Congo Republic were parties to an agreement about commercialization of their respective forests. This arrangement was a legacy of the AEF era when commercial control of Gabonese timber was in Brazzaville, the AEF capital. Friction between Gabon and Brazzaville over the disposition of Gabon's timber had been a long-standing issue, and after a series of disagreements between the two governments, the Gabonese assumed exclusive national control.

Until the late 1950s, *okoumé* and other woods were the major exports of the Gabonese economy. As late as 1960, 80 percent of the national budget represented income from the sale of *okoumé* and nearly forty firms engaged in the timber business. To support Gabon's entry into the lucrative plywood market spurred by the European building boom, SNBG encouraged the development of an extensive infrastructure of sawmills and plywood manufacturing facilities at Port Gentil. The facilities of Gabon's largest and most influential forestry firm, the Compagnie forestière du

TABLE 3.1   Timber Production and Value of Timber Exports, 1985–1990

	1985	1986	1987	1988	1989	1990
Timber production (000 m³)						
Okoumé	977	957	868	989	944	1,046[a]
Ozigo	49	56	39	52	48	58
Other species	212	219	200	200	200	337
Total	1,238	1,232	1,107	1,241	1,192	1,537[b]
Value of timber exports (F CFA bn)						
Okoumé logs	34.6	30.7	31.2	32.5	36.5	40.1[a]
Other logs	14.9	12.0	—	—	6.9	10.1[a]
Manufactured products	6.2	5.9	—	—	6.5	4.7[a]
Total	55.7	48.6	46.9	48.3	49.9	54.9[a]

[a]January-November.
[b]Estimates.

Source: Economist Intelligence Unit (EIU) Country Profile, *Gabon, Equatorial Guinea, 1991–92*, p. 14. Reprinted by permission of EIU, London.

Gabon (CFG), at Port Gentil are among the most advanced in the world for plywood construction.[7]

In the late 1960s, Gabonese wood exports began a precipitous decline. More than 85 percent of the timber harvested in Gabon is exported, and unfortunately for the Gabonese, substantial production and transportation costs make Gabon's wood products expensive in the traditional European markets. Competition from Malaysia and other Asian countries has cut into European imports from Gabon and effectively dampened Gabonese hopes to enhance their place in the world market (see Table 3.1).

Although SNBG has had some success in developing new markets in Israel, Hong Kong, and India, Gabon's export market retains its historical orientation toward the metropole, to the commercial disadvantage of the Gabonese. By 1988, *okoumé* and other wood products represented only 7 percent of Gabon's total exports and 6 percent of export earnings. The reversal of the market has also damaged the fortunes of the SNBG, which has reported losses for the past several years and lost the participation of the Belgians in the consortium.[8]

Fortunately for the Gabonese, the sharp increase in the OPEC price for petroleum in the early 1970s more than compensated for the diminished wood exports. By the late 1970s, petroleum had replaced *okoumé* as the mainstay of Gabon's export market and had become the major source of income for the Gabonese treasury. The shift was dramatic: Between 1972 and the OPEC oil embargo in 1974, the price of Gabonese crude oil increased 300 percent. In only two years, the production of Gabonese crude rose from 7.5 million to 10.2 million metric tons with an increase in income that more than offset the losses from the depressed plywood market.[9]

Exploration for petroleum in Gabon was begun in the early 1930s by the French national oil company, the Compagnie française des petroles (CFP), and continued after World War II by a regional affiliate, the Société des petroles de l'Afrique équatoriale française (SPAEF). Following the era of colonial independence in 1960, the restructured and renamed national French oil company Elf Aquitaine, by agreement with the Gabonese government, became the major producer of Gabonese petroleum.

After many years of exploration, the first significant find was by SPAEF at Ozouri in 1957. Ozouri is located in a major petroleum field in the general vicinity of Port Gentil and Cap Lopez along the Atlantic coast south of Libreville. After the discovery of the major Grondin field in 1967, production shifted increasingly to offshore sites with corresponding increases in production costs. The discovery of the first major offshore site, Gamba-Ivinga, in 1974 represented a major turning point in the production of Gabonese petroleum. Between 1972 and 1974, the tonnage of crude oil from the offshore sites surpassed production from the mainland wells. Until the discovery of Gamba-Ivinga and movement to the offshore sites, Elf Gabon, the Gabonese subsidiary of Elf Aquitaine, monopolized production. A critical decision at this time by the Gabonese government to increase production led to the entry of British, U.S., and Japanese firms into the petroleum business in Gabon. Shell Gabon was followed by the U.S. firm Gulf Gabon, and within several years a dozen firms, among them the major U.S. companies American Oil Company (AMOCO) and Tenneco, were involved in exploration and production of Gabonese crude. Despite the entry of the newcomers, Elf Gabon's percentage of total production remains nearly 70 percent. Elf Gabon is also involved in the refining and marketing of petroleum: the Compagnie *Gabon-Elf* de raffinage (COGER) refines petroleum for the markets of western Europe with the central African market being served by a second refinery in Port Gentil operated by the Société gabonaise de raffinage (SOGARA). The fortunes of both COGER and SOGARA declined dramatically in the mid-1980s due to the precipitous decline of oil prices in Europe and the installation of refineries in Cameroon and the Congo Republic that ended Gabon's virtual monopoly of these neighboring markets (see Table 3.2). Production of natural gas, often found in conjunction with petroleum, has paralleled developments in petroleum exploration and production in Gabon. An average annual production of 72 million metric tons between 1986 and 1989 provides an additional dimension to Gabon's economy.[10]

In 1981, alarm arose over the relatively rapid depletion of Gabon's petroleum reserves: At the production levels of that period, Gabon could

TABLE 3.2   Petroleum Production, 1989–1991 (000 barrels per day)

	Jan.-Mar.	Apr.-Jun.	Jul.-Sept.	Oct.-Dec.
1989	177	197	223	273
1990	267	258	277	300
1991	300[a]	150[b]		

[a]Average for two months.
[b]Estimate.

Source: Economist Intelligence Unit (EIU) Country Report, Congo, Gabon, Equatorial Guinea, no. 3, 1991, Appendix. Reprinted by permission of EIU, London.

expect to exhaust its reserves within fifteen years. The prospects for a continuing prosperity based on petroleum earnings were considerably enhanced by Shell Gabon's discovery in 1985 of the Rabi-Kounga field south of Port Gentil. Rabi-Kounga is the largest onshore deposit yet found in Gabon; the combined field is estimated at 160 million metric tons—approximately 1.2 billion barrels—with the expectation that 450 million barrels, or 37.5 percent, can be commercialized in the next decade. Shell's soundings have confirmed that Rabi-Kounga is, in fact, part of an even larger onshore field in the Sette Cama basin that could dwarf Gabon's known reserves.[11]

As the world's thirtieth leading producer of petroleum, and the fourth largest in Africa, after Nigeria, Libya, and Algeria, Gabon plays an important role in world production of petroleum. As a member of OPEC, the government of Gabon participates in deliberations about worldwide production and pricing of petroleum. Despite the decline in the OPEC price of crude oil in the 1980s, demand for petroleum is increasing in the traditional industrial markets as well as a number of areas of the Third World. An increase in demand may not, however, serve Gabon's long-term interests. Even if the Rabi-Kounga field expands Gabon's petroleum reserves as anticipated, the country's economic well-being will continue to depend on a nonrenewable resource. Although the search continues for new onshore and offshore sites, the government is aware that its dependency on petroleum is inherently risky. The situation is, in fact, akin to Gabon's earlier, critical dependency on okoumé. In an effort to create a more diversified economy, beginning in 1966, the government developed a series of economic plans to offset the distortions inherent in a "single-crop" economy. Using its extensive revenues from petroleum, the government embarked on the Transgabonais railway, its most ambitious project and the cornerstone of a policy of diversification as well as the primary objective of the first five-year economic plan.

ECONOMIC DIVERSIFICATION:
THE TRANSGABONAIS

The dream of a rail system to bring products from the remote, inaccessible areas of the country is a long-standing one. De Brazza spoke of the merits of a rail line to the Congo basin and, in 1905, AEF Commissioner Emile Gentil commissioned the French engineer Cambrier to undertake the study of a rail link between Libreville and the Ivindo basin—a distance of a thousand kilometers (over 600 miles). In 1912, AEF Governor-General Martial Merlin, echoing de Brazza, proposed a railway that would link the Congo basin with the Gabonese capital. Successive administrations concluded that the cost of a project of such scale was simply prohibitive. The question of constructing a railway was raised again in the mid-1950s in conjunction with plans by U.S. Steel to develop the iron ore deposits in the northeast near Bélinga. In 1968, following Bongo's accession to the presidency and positive feasibility studies by French and U.S. engineering firms, the government made the decision to construct the Transgabonais railway. In 1969, the government invited international participation in the project, creating a special fund, Groupement européen pour la construction du chemin de fer transgabonais (EUROTRAG) for national and international investments. French interests represent nearly 40 percent of EUROTRAG's participation, followed by British firms at 22 percent. The total EUROTRAG consortium brought together nearly twenty firms specializing in various aspects of the construction project. Major international funding agencies like the World Bank and the IMF refused to participate on grounds that the project remained too much of an undertaking, especially for Gabon's resources.

Clearly, the decision to begin construction of the Transgabonais was controversial. Critics of the project argued that an efficient road-water network could be constructed for a fraction of the cost of the railway. When fully completed, the Transgabonais will cost nearly U.S.$5 billion but to many Gabonese, the political and economic value of the project is well worth the cost. The Transgabonais is, in fact, a stunning feat of civil engineering. In the construction of the railway, supervised by the Office de chemin de fer transgabonais (OCTRA), over 3000 workers were employed in building a major tunnel at Junkville and the bridges required to cross the difficult terrain. The project involved the deforestation of thousands of acres of dense tropical forests with a virtual armada of mechanized equipment.

The path of the Transgabonais can be viewed as a Y turned on its side, with the trunk of the Y extending from the station at Owendo (the port of Libreville) to Booué at the confluence of the Ogooué and Ivindo

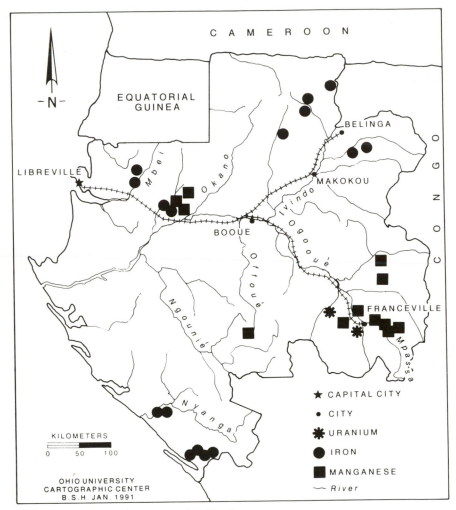

FIGURE 3.1   Mineral Deposits and Railroad

rivers (see Figure 3.1). From Booué, one line of the Y branches north toward the iron ore deposits at Bélinga; the other line of the Y is directed toward the manganese and uranium deposits in the south near Franceville, the southern terminus of the railway. Until the construction of the Trans-gabonais, manganese, for example, was shipped to the coast by way of the neighboring Congo Republic with a corresponding vulnerability that the Gabonese never accepted with equanimity. Similarly, exports of iron ore from Bélinga in the northeast—geologists estimate deposits in excess of a billion tons—would be facilitated by the more efficient linkage with the coast. The Owendo-Booué segment of the line was inaugurated in

1983 in a ceremony attended by French President Mitterrand, and the Booué-Franceville section is partially completed. Critics of the project found ample ammunition in the performance of the line in its first years, but the situation has improved with increased shipments of manganese and an increase in the volume of timber now being shipped by rail. In 1988, passenger and cargo fees produced a revenue of U.S.$35 million, more than one-half the U.S.$60 million needed to make the line self-supporting and a substantial increase over its earnings of U.S.$20 million in 1987. In 1989, freight shipments represented nearly 80 percent of the total revenue produced by the line; in its first few years of operation, the Transgabonais was reported to carry fewer passengers than the national airline, Air Gabon.[12]

According to Pierre Péan, the Transgabonais is an important component in Bongo's personal political strategy; upon completion of the Transgabonais, Bongo will, according to Péan, propose a shift of the capital from Libreville to Franceville, the southern terminus of the railway and the home of Gabon's Batéké population. Péan asserted that Bongo aspires to be recognized as the King of the Batékés and to return in triumph on the Transgabonais to claim his crown.

It is not likely that the Transgabonais will accomplish all that is expected of it, and Péan's *Affaires africaines* is clearly an unsympathetic treatment of the Bongo regime. Péan is correct, however, in pointing out that the Transgabonais has enhanced Bongo's power and authority throughout the country. Many Gabonese are fiercely proud of the accomplishment and view it as an important expression of national sovereignty. In this context, it is an important achievement. The more remote regions of the country are now linked to events and activities of the nation, and travel from many areas of the interior to Libreville has been reduced from days to hours.

In conjunction with building the Transgabonais, the government intensified efforts to exploit other sources of wealth, with the expressed goal of reducing dependency on petroleum. With the Transgabonais providing the transportation component, the government could look to the nation's vast mineral resources as the next critical step in its development strategy.

MINING

After petroleum, the production of manganese is the government's highest priority. Extensive deposits of manganese are located in the Batéké region at Moanda, near Franceville. The Moanda deposits represent 20 percent of the known deposits in the world, and 25 percent of manganese deposits outside the Soviet Union. Until the construction of the Transgabonais, manganese was shipped to the coast on the world's longest *téléphérique*, an aerial conveyor belt 74 km (46 mi) long, and Congo Rail, which carried the manganese from the terminus of the *téléphérique* at Mbinda in the Congo to the Congo port of Pointe Noire for continuing transit. The completion of the Transgabonais and the opening of a new French-built mineral port at Owendo will provide a more direct, and possibly more economical, route to the coast.

Manganese production is handled by an investment company similar to that formed to develop and market petroleum. The major owners of the joint investment company COMILOG are U.S. Steel, which holds 34.6 percent of the shares; the French firm Compagnie française des mines (CFM), which controls 17.6 percent; and the Gabonese government and Gabonese private investors who together own approximately 30 percent of the shares. Manganese production is just behind that of the USSR and South Africa, ranking Gabon as the third leading producer of the world's manganese (see Table 3.3).[13]

Manganese is used in the production of heat-resistant alloys and is an integral component in the production of steel. Thus, the market for manganese is intimately related to conditions in the steel industry. In the past decade, Gabonese production slowed in concert with the steel industry in the United States and western Europe; as for petroleum, the declining price of manganese reflected the U.S. dollar's rapid drop in value between 1986 and 1988. Gabonese profits from the sale of manganese declined in 1987 to F CFA 55 million (U.S.$204,000) from a reported profit of F CFA 1.5 billion (U.S.$5.5 million) in 1986. Manganese is, after petroleum and wood products, the third leading earner of export income; in 1988, manganese sales represented approximately 8 percent of Gabon's total exports. Agreements with China and the Philippines to purchase manganese are expected to provide some stability in both production and revenue. Looking toward new uses for manganese, a U.S. firm, Schotte Pellet Technologies of Pittsburgh, is studying the feasibility of using Pennsylvania coal in a projected ferromanganese fusion plant at Moanda.[14]

In addition to major deposits of manganese, Gabon boasts a substantial supply of uranium. The largest deposits are in the Haut-Ogooué region, in an area called the plateau of the Batéké near Franceville. Mining of uranium is the exclusive responsibility of the Compagnie des mines de Franceville (COMUF), which had until 1974 only one customer, the Commissariat à l'energie atomique, the French atomic energy agency. In fact, the initial capital for the development of Gabon's uranium reserves was provided by this agency, whose Gabonese subsidiary, the Compagnie générale de matières nucléaires (COGEMA), is the direct owner of 18.8 percent of the stock in COMUF.[15]

TABLE 3.3 Production and Exports of Manganese Ore and Uranium Metal, 1985–1990

	1985	1986	1987	1988	1989	1990[a]
Manganese ore						
Production (mn tons)	2.32	2.51	2.59	2.25	2.55	2.42
Exports (mn tons)	2.23	2.48	2.29	2.93	2.60	1.68
Exports (F CFA bn)	49.5	38.2	32.4	45.0	60.2	54.0
Average fob price (F CFA 000/ton)	22.2	15.4	14.2	15.4	22.0	31.2
Uranium metal						
Production (tons)	439	900	744	929	862	709
Exports (tons)	900	857	857	902	900	707
Exports (F CFA bn)	27.9	25.5	24.0	22.1	21.2	14.4
Average fob price (F CFA 000/ton)	31.0	29.7	28.0	24.5	23.6	20.3

[a]Estimates.

Source: Economist Intelligence Unit (EIU) Country Profile, *Gabon, Equatorial Guinea, 1991–92*, pp. 15, 16. Reprinted by permission of EIU, London.

In a classic example of colonial economics, uranium is not used in Gabon; until 1974, its production was reserved for France's military and civilian nuclear energy projects, notably the *force de frappe* (nuclear striking force) and electricity generation. After the nuclear accident at Chernobyl in the Soviet Union in 1986, Bongo cancelled a project to develop a Gabonese reactor with the assistance of the French. The reactor had been part of the price for normal relations with France exacted by Bongo at the conclusion of the Péan affair in 1984 but the addition of a nuclear reactor to generate electricity in Gabon was not urgent. Hydroelectric facilities in several areas of the country, principally at Kinguelé, on the Mbei River, appear to provide an adequate supply of electricity throughout the country despite an increasing demand for residential and commercial air conditioning. In this context, the Ogooué and its major tributaries satisfy yet another important dimension of Gabon's basic economic needs. In 1974, Gabon renegotiated cooperation agreements with France that ended exclusive French rights to its uranium. Gabon's buyers now include Japan, Italy, and Belgium. COGEMA's share of production, nearly 60 percent, constitutes 9 percent of France's national demand for uranium. Since 1980, the U.S. firm Union Carbide has been actively exploring for new uranium deposits.

In addition to manganese and uranium, Gabon's hopes for economic diversity rest precariously on the promise represented by major iron ore deposits in the northeast, near Bélinga. Unfortunately, the deposits are located at some distance from major population centers and existing road and water transportation. Further development of these deposits depends on completion of the Booué-Bélinga stage of the Transgabonais. In the current constrained budgetary environment, the government may delay this decision for some time, but it was reported in 1990 that with the assistance of Chinese capital and technical assistance, Gabon looked to an early completion of this phase of the project.

The precious metals that captured the imagination of earlier explorers retain little significance in the contemporary Gabonese economy. Exploration for gold continues by individual prospectors with production reported to be only a few hundred kilograms (several hundred pounds) per year. Prospecting for diamonds is limited to regional production, although a European consortium, the Société européene de diamant d'investissement au Gabon (EDI-GABON), plans expansion. Gabon's modern economy rests on its ability to provide primary resources indispensable for contemporary industrial development. The discovery of several "modern" minerals—titanium, niobium, rare earths, and phosphates—opens possibilities for diversification in the mineral sector.[16]

The extractive industries, in conjunction with the construction of the Transgabonais, represent significant efforts to create the foundation of a modern, diversified economy. Although there are inevitable market uncertainties, the government, particularly with its decision to build the Transgabonais, has taken immense steps in the direction of diversification. Although each step may, in fact, increase dependency on foreigners by markedly increasing indebtedness, the government's apparent attempt to create an equilibrium between self-sufficiency and dependency is an intriguing gamble. In the traditional agricultural sector, efforts have been noticeably less successful.

AGRICULTURE

Gabonese agriculture provides a vivid illustration of the long-term effects of colonial economics. Gabon currently imports 80 percent of its food, creating a dependence on foreign supply and a corresponding exodus of a significant portion of its national income. The logging and mining industries have transformed the rural population into a semiurbanized proletariat dependent on imports of basic foodstuffs for its existence. A key factor in this transformation is the marked decrease in the area of cultivated land, recently estimated at only 0.5 percent of the total national territory.[17] Between 1960 and 1975, the area of cultivation dropped from 106,000 hectares (260,000 acres) to 73,000 (180,000 acres), a decrease of 32 percent. During this same period, demographic change in Gabon's villages reflected the flight of its most active members to the wage economy. By 1975, nearly 80 percent of the rural population was more than forty years old—a feature of rural life directly related to the decline in cultivated land during the preceding fifteen years. Despite government efforts to revitalize the rural sector, there has been no appreciable return of population to the villages.

The net result of decades of demographic shifts toward participation in the "modern" economy has been a profound depletion of the agricultural labor force and chronic inefficiency in agricultural production. Gabon's villages are home to the youngest and oldest members of the population, with more than half of Gabon's population residing in urbanized settings. Although half of Gabon's population is involved in agriculture, both age and the geographical distribution of the population create a situation that resists government efforts to increase agricultural production. Strong emphasis on agricultural development in five successive economic plans has failed to stimulate domestic production of foodstuffs.[18] In the mid-1960s, for example, with funds from the African Development Bank, the government sponsored a major project at Medouneu in the Woleu N'Tem to produce fruits and vegetables. Funds were allocated for road construction and maintenance in an effort to insure the delivery of the produce to Libreville and other regional markets, and the government provided technical and financial assistance to farmers who agreed to participate in this ambitious effort at self-reliance. In circumstances reminiscent of the nineteenth century, the project collapsed. Failure to maintain the road network made it virtually impossible to deliver highly perishable fresh fruits and vegetables to markets; many of the farmers participated only halfheartedly, and continuing problems of crop disease led to the abandonment of the project. Similar efforts to stimulate the production of pineapples and plantain bananas have met little success. A government-sponsored project at N'Toum, east of Libreville, failed after an expenditure of more than F CFA 1 billion (U.S.$3.7 million). Fraud, rumored to be widespread in the economy, may have been a factor here, as well as difficulties with transportation.[19]

Transportation is the Achilles' heel of Gabonese economic development. The road network, particularly the north-south axis, is virtually impassable during the rainy seasons. Intense rainfall and violent tropical storms pose major hazards to travelers and traffic on the roads. In 1981, the government ordered the development of an all-weather road network. A plan to construct a macadamized road connecting Libreville with Port Gentil was a major victim of the austerity program of the late 1980s, and travel between Gabon's major cities and many interior locations remains hazardous and difficult. Despite the government's occasional efforts to upgrade the road system, only 510 km (315 mi), or 6.5 percent, of the nation's total road system of 7,800 km (4,800 mi) were paved by 1986.[20]

Nor have the problems been alleviated by the construction of the Transgabonais; its route does not include the larger towns of the eastern coastal regions. In an ambitious effort to compensate for its difficulties in surface transportation, the government developed a number of regional airports and landing facilities around the country. The Léon Mba airport at Libreville is the hub of an air system that provides regular flights to Port Gentil, Lambaréné, and Franceville. Additionally, several hundred modest landing strips are used by logging and mining firms to reach some of the more inaccessible areas of the country. Although this air network facilitates travel, it is a totally inadequate substitute for an all-weather road network suitable for transporting substantial volumes of goods efficiently and economically throughout the country.

Gabon's problems of agricultural production are compounded by the topography of the country. Rain forests cover 85 percent of the country, and some areas remain virtually inaccessible—thus, the significance of the Transgabonais. This conflict between the goal of self-sufficiency and the realities of geography and climate are readily apparent in another area of primary concern to the government: Gabon imports virtually all of its fresh meat and dairy products, and the prices charged for these products limit their distribution throughout the population. Most of the fresh meat consumed in Gabon comes from Cameroon, South Africa (in violation of the sanctions imposed by the Organization for African Unity), and Zimbabwe. Several highly subsidized ranches operated by the Société de développement de l'agriculture et de l'élevage au Gabon (AGROGABON) have experienced only marginal success in creating a domestic cattle industry. Gabon and its most immediate neighbors, the Congo Republic and Cameroon, suffer from infestations of the tse-tse fly and diseases that decimate herds of cattle with amazing rapidity. AGROGABON now raises cattle imported from the Ivory Coast that are reported to be immune to many of the traditional sicknesses. This innovation, which may permit Gabon to meet its needs for fresh meats and dairy products, represents an important symbolic break as well in the historic pattern of dependency. But for the short term, the accumulated problems mean a continuing reliance on imported foodstuffs. In 1988, the government further demonstrated this dependency in initiating an agreement with Morocco for the provision of fruits and vegetables.

As part of its effort to rejuvenate the agricultural sector, the government determined in its third five-year economic plan (1976–1980) to highlight the development of several traditional products: cocoa, coffee, palm oil, ground nuts, rubber, coconuts, and sugar cane. At least four of these—cocoa, coffee, palm oil, and rubber appear to have potential for both reducing imports and increasing Gabonese consumption of locally grown and produced commodities.

Cocoa production, which began in the late nineteenth century, is negligible in the international market, but plays a valuable role in the economic stability of the Woleu N'Tem, the bastion of Gabon's Fang population. Cocoa is currently the responsibility of the Société nationale de développement industrielle (SONADECI), created in 1978 to coordinate agricultural development. With government funds and more than U.S.$5 million from the CCCE and the African Development Bank, SONADECI launched an ambititous cocoa development project in several key population centers, the traditional cocoa-growing areas of Oyem, Mitzic, Bitam, and Minzoul. Between 1970, when the project began, and 1978, cocoa production increased slightly to an average of more than 5,000 tons per year.[21] Since 1981, production has declined, largely due to a depressed world price and serious problems of cultivation and transportation in the Woleu N'Tem. Cocoa plants are highly susceptible to disease, and the usual weather problems and inadequate road system limited access to the fields. Overall, the project can be considered moderately successful: The average income in the Woleu N'Tem is the highest in the rural areas of the country. The program's modest success is due also to government purchases of cocoa to stabilize the price paid to producers. In this instance, the political and economic benefits of the program, that is, stability in the

Woleu N'Tem, came into direct conflict with the financial austerity that began in 1986. By 1987, the government found itself in a difficult situation with respect to the world price for cocoa and the price it paid to producers. Losses averaged nearly F CFA 75,000 (U.S.$278) per ton and declining world consumption, with corresponding decreases in the price of cocoa, could seriously threaten the future of Gabonese production as well as the political tranquility of the Woleu N'Tem.[22]

The government similarly attempted to increase coffee production. As in the case of cocoa, Gabon's production of coffee is quite modest. Topography is the limiting factor: Coffee grows in only the three regions Ogooué-Ivindo, Ogooué-Lolo, and the Haut-Ogooué. In the past, the coffee crop suffered from the rural exodus and subsequent neglect, and despite rising coffee prices since 1970, production has not overcome this legacy. Government efforts to revitalize production have been similar to those for cocoa. The Caisse de stabilization de prix de café provides subsidies and purchases coffee from producers at a price considerably higher than the market price. But coffee will never become a major export commodity; the Gabonese can only hope that coffee, like cocoa production will provide regional economic stability. To the extent that production is sustained artificially by government subsidies and purchases, production will remain dependent on the overall health of the economy.

The production of palm oil is a traditional activity of Gabon's rural population. Prior to independence, several foreign firms, including the British conglomerate Unilever, were involved in palm oil production. In 1975, the government created the joint investment company, AGROGA-BON to manage palm oil production as well as other development projects. In the southeastern city of Lambaréné, AGROGABON operates two refineries and manages approximately 1,400 hectares (3,500 acres) of palm trees. From 1969 until 1975, production steadily increased and the project appeared to have a promising future. Then production unexpectedly declined in the next few years despite substantial financial assistance from the CCCE, the Gabonese Development Bank, and several European lenders. The project may have been a victim of the government's extensive budget for the OAU conference in Libreville in 1977; several development projects were reported to have been canceled or postponed when the government decreed a period of austerity to recover from its OAU spending spree. Despite the infrastructure now in place, the government continues to import large quantities of palm oil, and there is no indication that any substantial increase in production is likely in the near future.

After a delay of almost ten years, the government, with the assistance of the African Development Bank and the CCCE, initiated a major rubber production project in the Woleu N'Tem in 1985, subsequently expanded in 1989. The project is the responsibility of Hévéa-Gabon and is designed to restore Gabon's neglected rubber industry to a competitive state. The project covers almost 8,000 hectares (20,000 acres) and represents an initial investment of approximately U.S.$117 million. Determination of the success or failure of the project will not be possible for a number of years, as the peak period of rubber production is eighteen years after the seedlings are planted. In any case, it is not likely that Gabon will ever become a major exporter; rather, rubber production holds the limited promise of regional economic stability in the manner of cocoa and coffee.

One area of agricultural production that illustrates some success is rice production, a project begun during the AEF era, but limited by problems of transportation and a supposed Gabonese preference for manioc. In 1969, with the assistance of the Chinese and the African Development Bank, the government inaugurated a new effort to stimulate rice production in the traditional rice-growing areas near Tchibanga and N'Dendé in the south. Domestic production now accounts for approximately 40 percent of the rice consumed in the country. The consumption of manioc, one of the staples of the rural diet, appears to be declining with the increasing urbanization of the population.

Poultry farming, albeit limited, is also a relatively successful area of the agricultural sector. The government, with the usual technical and financial involvement of a French firm, invested substantial sums in the development of a local poultry industry. The Société industrielle d'agriculture et d'élevage de Boumango (SIAE) raises poultry for local markets previously monopolized by imports from France and other Common Market countries. Domestic production now meets 50 percent of the national demand, representing one of the rare successes in the effort to reduce the country's dependency on imports.[23]

These cases illustrate several fundamental problems that confound agricultural planners in Gabon. First, the realities of climate and geography weigh heavily on any effort to bolster agricultural production, a situation exacerbated by the flight to the cities that with the exception of the Woleu N'Tem has left many of Gabon's rural areas virtually empty. Gabon's most active population now resides in dozens of small and moderately sized towns and the three major population centers, Libreville, Port Gentil, and Franceville. In an effort to compensate for the relatively few Gabonese available for agricultural work, the government relies on farm laborers from other African countries. Reliance on foreign labor creates its own risks in periods of economic austerity or depression, and the government's practice of identifying scapegoats in the expatriate community during periods of economic difficulty has produced tension and violence. It may be that the government and the people of Gabon will have to reconcile themselves to their economic predicament: Gabon is an underpopulated country with an active labor force that is oriented to an urban style and standard of living. It seems unlikely that anything less than a major economic depression would change this reality.

MANUFACTURING AND CONSTRUCTION

Gabon's manufacturing infrastructure reflects the importance of petroleum, logging, and mining to the national economy. Representing approximately 7 percent of GNP, petroleum refining and timber processing form the foundation of manufacturing activity. At Pointe Clairette, near Port Gentil, SOGARA operates two refineries that supply the bulk of Gabon's domestic petroleum needs. The Port Gentil area is also the site of several plants involved in the manufacture of plywood and other wood products. Plans to construct a major cellulose plant to produce paper products were abandoned in 1983 after the government failed to secure funding. With initial funding from the CCCE, the government operates two cement factories, whose fortunes are declining in concert with the general recession affecting the Gabonese economy. Production of cement for domestic use dropped from 211,000 tons in 1986 to 137,000 tons in 1989. Prompted by agreements with the IMF to encourage small and medium-sized businesses, the government has encouraged diversification in this sector of the economy. Since 1987, funds have been provided from internal and external sources for investments in breweries, mineral water bottling, and sugar refining; a new pharmaceutical factory geared to a central African market was opened in 1989. Additional funds for diversification in the industrial sector are provided by a special investment fund created in 1974; the Provision pour investissements diversifiés (PID) calls upon foreign firms to contribute at least 2 percent of their profits to the effort to create a more diversified domestic manufacturing sector. PID funds have contributed to the development of a domestic paint industry, cement production, and an ambitious effort to restore the palm oil industry to its earlier status. Although the erratic performance of petroleum in the 1980s limited the funds available for investment, the government appears determined to implement its diversification strategy in the manufacturing sector.

The overall health of the Gabonese construction industry is a direct reflection of the government's twenty-year effort to complete the Transgabonais rail system. Expenditures on the Transgabonais amount to the single largest expenditure for construction projects, followed by the construction of the long-awaited mineral port at Owendo, which was formally inaugurated in 1988.[24]

FOREIGN TRADE AND COMMERCE

Gabon's economy relies on the performance of its major export commodities in the world and regional markets. Petroleum, wood, manganese, and uranium are the backbone of Gabon's export trade. In earnings, petroleum far exceeds the others and in total volume, exceeds the other three commodities combined. The simple truth is that despite concerted efforts on the part of the government to achieve diversification, petroleum remains the foundation of Gabon's economy. Completion of the first stages of the Transgabonais has clearly benefited the production of timber products and manganese, although the decision to postpone the Booué-Bélinga phase will limit the plans for expanded iron ore production and transportation to the mineral port at Owendo. The limited market for uranium will probably continue into the near future.

Volatility in the petroleum market creates a precarious condition with respect to the balance between exports and imports. In the past decade, the decline in exports has been accompanied by net increases in imports, and the resulting dependency on imported goods and services continues to plague the economy. Although some diversification in the pattern of exports and imports has taken place, France remains Gabon's pivotal economic partner. Canada and the United States are steadily increasing their purchases of Gabonese products, principally petroleum: In 1988, exports to the United States and Canada combined represented 27.3 percent of Gabon's total exports. France received 36 percent of Gabon's exports and provided Gabon with 53 percent of its imported goods and services. In comparison, Canada and the United States together provided Gabon with only 10 percent of its imports, primarily heavy construction equipment. It is important to emphasize that the increasing volume of Gabonese exports purchased by Canada and the United States represent purchases of petroleum and manganese. Gabonese petroleum acquired new significance in the United States following the loss of large quantities of petroleum provided by Iran before the Khomeini revolution.[25]

COMMERCIAL FISHING

An area of the Gabonese economy that seemed to represent considerable promise, but has proved disappointing, is the fishing industry. One would assume that Gabon's waters would provide a steady livelihood for a number of its people, and, in fact, the fishing industry is a continuing puzzle for Gabonese planners. At one level, the relatively modest returns in this sector of the economy must be seen as the result of fierce international competition in the Gulf of Guinea; the Gabonese have simply ceded their place in the contest to other countries with more advanced industrial fishing technology. In 1969, after a number of years of apparent success, the Gabonese whale fishing industry, established before World War II, simply abandoned its place to more advanced whaling fleets from Japan and the Soviet Union. In 1986, the government entered into an agreement with the European Economic Community (EEC) to allow fishing fleets from several European countries to expand their activities in Gabon's territorial waters. Commercial fishermen from many other countries, accompanied by modern refrigeration trawlers, also regularly fish Gabon's waters, and even the neighboring Congo Republic funds commercial fishing at a significantly higher level than the Gabonese government.

Several major deficiencies seem to account for the modesty of Gabon's efforts in this potentially profitable area. There is, initially, a major shortage of refrigeration facilities for storage at sea and in the ports along the Atlantic coast. As in other sectors of the economy, the absence of a rapid means of distribution to the interior limits the market for seafood to the coastal cities. Investigators have concluded that commercial fishing of tuna is a potentially profitable venture, however, and the government has taken some initial steps in this area. Fishing in the Gulf of Guinea is not without its dangers. Gabonese fishermen have skirmished regularly with fishermen from Equatorial Guinea, and increasing the Gabonese presence in the gulf could heighten tensions between Gabon and other countries that routinely and aggressively fish these waters. In 1972, Gabon attempted to protect its small fishing industry by declaring an economic zone that extends 170 miles out into the Atlantic. The decision provoked the Macias regime in Equatorial Guinea to charge a violation of its territorial sovereignty, and Gabonese fishermen were attacked by Guineans. The dispute was mediated by a commission of the OAU, and the matter was resolved peacefully, although friction between the two governments continued until the overthrow of Macias in 1979. At the moment, there is little danger of any major confrontation, due to the limited capability of the Gabonese commercial fleet and the even more limited capability of the small Gabonese navy to enforce restrictions.

TOURISM

In 1977, the Bongo government hosted the annual conference of the OAU in Libreville. In a lavish display of its petroleum-based wealth, the government constructed a convention center designed to rival the most modern in the world. The Cité du 12 Mars, which includes a large conference and banquet center and housing for 1,650 visitors, was the focal point of the government's effort to attract regional and international conferences. Libreville's location on the estuary appears to provide an ideal location for the development of tourism. Bathers are protected by the outer banks of the estuary from the dangerous ocean currents that one encounters on other African beaches, and the construction of a number of modern hotels provides adequate infrastructure for a large tourist population. Since 1975, in Libreville alone, six major hotels have been constructed along the boulevard that parallels the oceanfront from the Léon Mba airport to the downtown government, business, and commercial area.

But Libreville is one of the world's most expensive cities, and old economic ghosts haunt the government's effort to develop the tourist industry. With Gabon's reliance on imports, the expense of providing and maintaining services demanded by Europeans limits the government's ambition to make Libreville a major African tourist center. Despite government subsidies to the hotels, tourists seeking modest accommodations, inexpensive restaurants, and so forth are consistently disappointed. In 1989, the average length of a tourist's stay in Gabon was 2.5 days, suggesting that most tourists cannot afford the relatively high cost of a Gabonese vacation. Although the Transgabonais will provide efficient transportation along its route, it remains difficult to reach popular attractions like the Albert Schweitzer hospital in Lambaréné, and the accommodations there, until the opening of a French-financed hotel in 1986, were quite limited.[26] The government's emphasis on economic development in such places as Franceville and Port Gentil will continue to attract a number of foreign tourists, but in all likelihood, the substantial cost of travel and accommodations will limit the development of a large tourist industry.

ECONOMIC REALITIES:
FROM BOOM TO AUSTERITY

After the rapid economic growth of the 1970s, demand for petroleum diminished in the mid-1980s with the decrease in the price of crude oil in the world and regional markets. Gabon's petroleum-export earnings fell from approximately U.S.$1.5 billion in 1975 to U.S.$800 million in 1986. In 1988, petroleum continued to account for 83 percent of Gabon's export revenue and 65 percent of the nation's total budget revenue—virtually the same proportion of the nation's revenue as *okoumé* in 1960. The decline in demand corresponded with a dramatic decline in the value of the U.S. dollar, the international petroleum currency, creating an immediate crisis for the Bongo government (see Table 3.4).

The government undertook a major budgetary review and imposed a severe austerity program in 1986. Bongo referred to Gabon's sudden, precarious situation as a financial Ramadan, with a corresponding need for abstinence and sacrifice. The national budget was reduced 11 percent

TABLE 3.4   Gross National Product, 1989 (% of total)

Agriculture and forestry	9.8
Mining	4.7
Petroleum and natural gas	31.1
Manufacturing and energy	10.3
Construction and public works	4.0
Trade, transport, and services	40.1

Source: Economist Intelligence Unit (EIU) Country Report, Congo, Gabon, Equatorial Guinea, no. 2, 1991, p. 5. Reprinted by permission of EIU, London.

with the elimination or postponement of major development projects and a serious revision in the fifth economic plan (1984–1988), which had proposed significant outlays for construction projects and agricultural development. The plan to build a new Foreign Affairs ministry building and the Booué-Bélinga section of the Transgabonais were major victims of the reduction. Additionally, the government imposed a 3 percent surtax, called a solidarity loan, on the salaries of civil servants. In December 1986, to satisfy conditions for a commitment by the IMF to assist in rescheduling payments on Gabon's U.S.$1.2 billion foreign debt—virtually all of it representing loans for the Transgabonais—the government imposed additional measures to limit spending. Subsidies to state-owned utilities were reduced and plans were made, in accordance with IMF guidelines, to privatize a number of state-owned firms, including the food distribution firm Société commerce et développement (CODEV), the state-owned gasoline distribution company Société nationale de distribution des produits pétroliers (PIZO), and the Société des transports de voyageurs de Libreville (SOTRAVIL), the urban transit firm that provides public transportation in Libreville and Port Gentil. Gabon's external debt has since attained U.S.$2.4 billion; the IMF, the World Bank, and the African Development Bank have provided additional funds to assist the government with its balance-of-payments problems and its commitment to continue its program of economic diversification. Adhering to the spirit of the IMF guidelines, Gabon's last three national budgets, for the years 1987–1990, have continued the initial 1986 reductions.

In a related move, the government initiated steps in 1989 to control the illegal, or "parallel" economy that exists outside the sanctioned framework of government planning and tax collection. A significant volume of smuggling is reported to occur, primarily across Gabon's borders with Cameroon and Equatorial Guinea. Strict immigration controls have been instituted to limit the illegal entry of workers, notably Guinean and Cameroonian Fang, as well as an array of commodities that flow across these borders without inspection or payment of duties. Estimates are that the parallel economy, reportedly dominated by non-Gabonese immigrants, could represent a loss of nearly F CFA 290 billion (over U.S.$1 billion) annually to the Gabonese treasury.[27]

As part of its commitment to the IMF, the government launched a major revision of its policies on salaries and wages in an effort to make the economy more competitive. Wages and salaries in both the public and private sectors are considerably higher in Gabon than in neighboring countries. In the 1988 budget, the government eliminated the traditional "thirteenth month" bonus for civil servants and adopted a plan to scale salaries down as much as 10 percent for persons earning more than F CFA 600,000 (U.S.$2,000) per month. All enterprises are expected to implement a 15 percent reduction in total wages. Salary and wage cuts have been accompanied by reductions in the size of the civil service through substantial layoffs and elimination of positions. Within this framework of salary and wage reductions, the issue of foreign workers takes on special significance. Gabonese workers receive F CFA 20,000 (U.S.$74) per month beyond the minimum wage for all workers of F CFA 44,000 (U.S.$163), making non-Gabonese African labor particularly attractive to employers in times of austerity.[28]

In general, efforts are being made to reduce the cost of public enterprises, and managers are under a strict mandate to make their enterprises profitable without the traditional government subsidies. In fact, the development of private enterprise is the hallmark of the IMF plan. As noted earlier, a number of initiatives are under way to reduce the direct expenditure of government funds for the operation of various activities. The IMF plan includes the development of more small and medium-sized businesses that would be truly private, and the government has launched an extensive review of its policies on investments and tariffs. Given Bongo's predisposition toward liberal investment policies and his repeated commitments to the tenets of a liberal economy, there is no apparent conflict between the free-market orientation of the IMF and the policies of the Bongo government. It is clear, however, that a significant number of Gabonese resent these severe austerity measures, and it is equally certain that the government's austerity program is a contributing cause of the continuing unrest in the country. On January 18, 1990, members of Gabon's usually docile labor federation, FESYGA, and students at the national university in Libreville engaged in public demonstrations against the continuation of these measures. Immediately following these demonstrations, the government restricted public meetings and expressions of discontent over official economic policies. Students were concerned about their scholarships and allowances, and FESYGA members were increasingly apprehensive about employment security and wages; in this context, competition from expatriate labor becomes critical. It is quite likely that Gabon's prosperity has produced expectations that the government may find difficult to satisfy in a climate of prolonged austerity. This situation, coupled with significant disenchantment with Bongo's authoritarian rule, is most certainly the foundation of the mounting opposition to the Bongo regime and the events of spring 1990.

The government's persistence in implementing the austerity program called for by the IMF facilitated an agreement with major creditors to provide relief in the repayment of Gabon's external debt. With the assistance of the French Ministry of Economics, the clubs of London and Paris, representing major lenders in the United States and Europe, agreed to a major rescheduling of Gabon's debt payments. In 1987, the clubs agreed to allow Gabon to reschedule principal and interest payments due in 1987 and 1988 over a ten-year period. Another of Gabon's major creditors, Japan, also agreed to prolonging the repayment of the approximately U.S.$25 million owed to Japanese banks, and Gabon received assistance from the French CCCE in 1987, and again in 1989, that will ease its repayment of a number of major loans for a variety of development projects sponsored by the CCCE.

The rescheduling relieved the government of an immediate source of anxiety, and Gabon faces a promising economic future. The international market for petroleum is improving, although efforts to expand the export of wood products and manganese are, at best, problematic. In any event, petroleum revenue must form the foundation for future diversification, and the economic fortunes of the country remain fundamentally dependent on that one product. After several years' decline, in 1989, the government received an increased production quota for petroleum from OPEC of approximately 9 percent. Given increasing demand, and continuing discoveries of major new reserves in the Rabi-Kounga field, Gabon can expect an adequate margin of protection for the foreseeable future.

A conservative assessment of the economy would no doubt conclude that the government has failed to achieve a number of its primary diversification goals. Gabon's dependence on imported goods and services remains as great as ever, Gabon's balance of payments is a continuing problem, and the contraction of petroleum production has had an overall dampening effect on economic growth. On the positive side of the ledger, one could conclude that Gabon's small population is blessed by one of the highest per capita incomes on the continent (U.S.$3,200), and that, in general, the standard of living for many Gabonese is superior to that of the vast majority of Africans. Measures of per capita income mask the critical issue of income distribution, however. A study of income distribution in Gabon published by the International Labour Office (ILO) in 1984 reported that 57.3 percent of the national income is earned by 20 percent of the population.[29] One observer, basing his comments on more recent UN data, reported the situation as even more extreme: Francis

Kpatindé wrote that 80 percent of the nation's wealth is in the hands of 2 percent of the population![30] Although the most egregious disparities in income of the early 1960s have been attenuated by the generalized prosperity of the boom years, the economic reality is that a few Gabonese are very rich and a substantial number very poor. The government itself raised the issue of income distribution in the fifth economic plan (1984–1989), although the plan neither provided details about the extent of maldistribution nor discussed any proposals to correct the problem.[31]

It is ironic that the mounting opposition to the Bongo regime corresponds with generally positive assessments of the Gabonese economy by such international arbiters of economic performance as the World Bank and the IMF, whose concern does not extend to the issue of income distribution. In early 1990, at approximately the same time as the disturbances in Libreville and Port Gentil, the Gabonese government received praise from the IMF for the success of its austerity program and its ongoing efforts to implement liberal economic policies. One can only pray that the discontent rising from the accumulated grievances against the Bongo regime, and exacerbated by the IMF requirements, do not, in continued expressions of fury, destroy the tentative and precarious preparations for a more democratic future.

Economically and politically, Gabon has made important changes in its relationship with France. Thirty years of independence have nurtured a strong sense of Gabonese nationalism, and the years of prosperity have widened Gabonese political and economic horizons. Bongo's appointment of Pierre Claver Maganga-Moussavou as an economic adviser suggests continuing uneasiness with the remaining Gabonese dependence on the French. Maganga-Moussavou is the author of an exhaustive study of Franco-Gabonese relationships between 1960 and 1978 that is sharply critical of historic French economic policies toward the former colonies. His general thesis is that *coopération* continues the outflow of Gabon's wealth and the real benefits derived from developing its resources. Maganga-Moussavou proposed to reduce dependency by reorienting Gabon's export policies and undertaking a substantial effort to revitalize the agricultural sector. Dependency is an intricate economic and psychological relationship, however. Gabon's ties to France transcend "merely" economic linkages, and France remains Gabon's point of reference despite occasional displays of mutual irritation. In his conclusion, Maganga-Moussavou underlined the need for Gabon to reorient both its economy and its approach to the world. If the Gabonese can accomplish these twin goals, they will break a chain of relationships that has endured since Bouët negotiated the initial Franco-Gabonese agreements with the *aga* of the left and right banks of the Gabon estuary.

NOTES

1. There is a detailed discussion of the agreements and economic dependency in Pierre Claver Maganga-Moussavou, *L'aide publique de la France au développement du Gabon depuis l'indépendance* (Paris: Publications de la Sorbonne, 1982). Debré's letter to Mba is cited on page 186. There is an abbreviated version of Maganga-Moussavou's study in English: *Economic Development: Does Aid Help? A Case Study of French Development Assistance to Gabon,* ed. Barbara J. Sims (Washington, D.C.: African Communications Liaison Service, 1983). The seminal study of Gabonese dependency on France is Joan Spero, *Dominance-Dependence Relationship: The Case of France and Gabon,* Ph.D. diss., Columbia University, 1973.

2. Maganga-Moussavou, *Economic Development: Does Aid Help?,* p. 147.

3. EIU Country Profile, *Gabon, Equatorial Guinea, 1991–92,* pp. 15–17.

4. CFA originally stood for Colonies françaises d'Afrique; and, after 1960, Communauté financière africaine.

5. Information on the FAC and CCCE is derived from Maganga-Moussavou, *L'aide publique de la France au Gabon depuis l'independence,* Part 2, Chapters 1–3; and "Gabon 1981," *Marchés tropicaux et méditérranéens* (special edition), 31, no. 1881 (November 27, 1981), pp. 3131–3132.

6. Organization for Economic Cooperation and Development (OECD), *Geographical Distribution of Financial Flows to Developing Countries* (Paris: OECD Publications Service, 1970–1986).

7. For a description of the timber industry, see Jacqueline Bouquerel, *Le Gabon* (Paris: Que sais-je?/Presses universitaires de France, 1976), pp. 68–82.

8. EIU Country Profile, *Gabon, Equatorial Guinea, 1991–92,* pp. 12–17.

9. EIU Country Profiles, *Gabon, Equatorial Guinea,* 1988–1992.

10. EIU Country Profile, *Gabon, Equatorial Guinea, 1991–92,* p. 5.

11. EIU Country Report, *Congo, Gabon, Equatorial Guinea,* no. 2 (1990).

12. James Brooke, "African Railroad Running A Deficit," *New York Times,* May 23, 1988, p. IV, 10:3.

13. Maganga-Moussavou, *L'aide publique de la France au Gabon depuis l'independence,* p. 287.

14. EIU Country Profile, *Gabon, Equatorial Guinea, 1989–90,* pp. 15–16.

15. Maganga-Moussavou, *L'aide publique de la France au Gabon depuis l'independence,* p. 287.

16. EIU Country Report, *Congo, Gabon, Equatorial Guinea,* no. 1 (1990), p. 30.

17. EIU Country Profile, *Gabon, Equatorial Guinea, 1990–91,* p. 15.

18. Ministère de l'éducation nationale de la république gabonaise, *Géographie et cartographie du Gabon,* (Paris: Editions classique d'expression française, 1981), pp. 48–51.

19. "Gabon 1981," *Marchés tropicaux et méditérranéens,* pp. 3042–3045.

20. United Nations Economic Commission for Africa, *African Statistical Yearbook, 1987,* p. 47-10.

21. For periodic reports on the government's development projects, see *Economie et finances: Revue du ministère de l'économie et des finances chargé de*

participation, published biannually by the Ministry of Economics, Libreville. Material in this section compiled from "Gabon 1981," *Marchés tropicaux et mediterranéens*; EIU Country Profiles, *Gabon, Equatorial Guinea, 1988–1991*.

22. EIU Country Report, *Congo, Gabon, Equatorial Guinea*, no. 4 (1989), pp. 14–18.

23. EIU Country Report, *Congo, Gabon, Equatorial Guinea*, no. 2 (1990), p. 13.

24. For a discussion of the origin and evolution of the PID, see Maganga-Moussavou, *L'aide publique de la France au Gabon depuis l'independence*, pp. 212–214; EIU Country Profile, *Gabon, Equatorial Guinea, 1991–92*, pp. 19–21.

25. For a summary account of the changing role of the United States in the Gabonese economy, see U.S. Department of Commerce, International Trade Administration, *Foreign Economic Trends and Their Implications for the United States: Gabon* (Washington, D.C.: Government Printing Office, 1989).

26. EIU Country Profile, *Gabon, 1989–90*, p. 21.

27. EIU Country Report, *Congo, Gabon, Equatorial Guinea*, no. 1 (1990), p. 28.

28. In December 1990, F CFA 270 equalled U.S.$1.00. The minimum wage for Gabonese workers is U.S.$237.00 per month; for non-Gabonese Africans, the minimum is U.S.$163.00 per month.

29. International Labour Organization, *L'emploi et répartion des revenus dans la république gabonaise* (Addis Ababa: International Labour Office, 1984).

30. Francis Kpatindé, "Le Gabon entre Bongo et les Bûcherons," *Jeune Afrique*, no. 1558 (November 7–13, 1990), p. 29.

31. The issue of income distribution is a delicate subject in Gabon, and the Gabonese government rarely provides income data to the international agencies that compile such information.

4

The Society

Gabon is a society in transition. Just entering its fourth decade as an independent nation, it appears, predictably perhaps, uneasy with itself and uncertain of its future. Serious ethnic divisions persist, including a deep-rooted apprehension by other groups of Fang intentions and their apparent readiness to establish national dominance. The efforts by the current regime to develop national goals and a national identity may inadvertently become victims of dismantling Gabon's one-party system. It should be acknowledged, however, that appeals to the people in the name of Gabonese nationalism have not always been made with noble intentions.

THE PEOPLE

The most basic fact about the Gabonese population—its size—is the most elusive. The results of the census of 1980 were withdrawn by the government after widespread charges of inaccuracy. Estimates of the number of Gabonese range from 900,000 to the officially asserted 1,300,000. The number of a nation's citizens being a criterion for international financial assistance could explain the regime's propensity to exaggerate the size of its population. Many observers suggest that the last accurate census was that undertaken in 1960 at the time of Gabon's independence which judged the population to be approximately 450,000. Gabon's population certainly remains modest, but nevertheless, of tremendous variety and complexity.

At the time of the Portuguese arrival in the fifteenth century, the disposition of the indigenous population differed substantially from the present-day configuration of ethnic groups. The arrival of traders and missionaries from Europe and the United States provoked a fundamental rearrangement of the ethnographic map. A movement of Bantu from the north and east into Gabon was followed by several migrations of groups toward the Gabon coast. Although it remains difficult to specify dates for

A Fang warrior of the Betsi clan, circa 1900 (photo courtesy of the Gabon National Archives).

these movements, the evidence suggests that major shifts in population occurred between the sixteenth and nineteenth centuries. Of these migrations, the appearance of Fang clans in the Woleu N'Tem and the estuary region was an event surpassed in significance only by the earlier arrival of the Portuguese in the estuary. The vast majority of the Fang arrived in Gabon from Cameroon to the north in a movement described by one witness as terrifying. The French-American explorer Paul du Chaillu, who observed the Fang advance toward the estuary region, wrote that the Fang were "intelligent, with highly developed commercial instincts, having none of the vices of the coastal tribes."[1] Du Chaillu noted that the Fang could be expected to overwhelm and absorb other groups they encountered on their movement toward the coast. In retrospect, he was certainly correct in foreseeing their principal role in the political and economic life of Gabon.

The movement of the Fang into the northern regions and their subsequent migrations to other parts of the country—although the center of their strength remains the Woleu N'Tem and the estuary region—give Gabon much of its contemporary character. The largest group in the country, the Fang represent one-third of the population of Gabon and the backbone of the agriculturally diverse and prosperous Woleu N'Tem

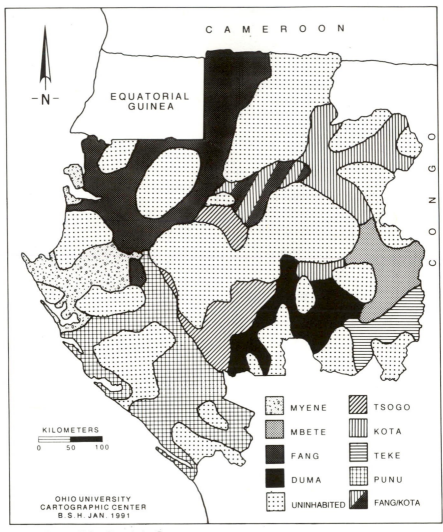

FIGURE 4.1   Ethnolinguistic Groups

region in the northernmost part of the country. In conjunction with their
kin in the southern part of neighboring Cameroon and Equatorial Guinea,
the Gabonese Fang are part of an ethnic family of nearly 800,000 persons
whose potential political power is a subject of substantial concern to the
current Gabonese leadership.

Including the Fang, there are nearly fifty ethnic groups in Gabon,
belonging to eight major linguistic families: Myéné (including Benga),
Kota, Duma, Tshogho, Mbété, Punu-Eshira, and Téké (see Figure 4.1).

Initial European contacts took place with Myéné-speaking groups that inhabited the estuary and the maritime areas of the Ogooué basin. These groups included the Mpongwé in the estuary region, the Orungu in the Ogooué delta around Port Gentil, the Nkomi in the Fernan Vaz, and the Galoa, Enenga, and Adjumba in the region of Lambaréné and the southern lakes. The Benga, who virtually disappeared in the nineteenth century, lived in relative isolation from the Mpongwé in the estuary, speaking a language uniquely their own. The remaining Benga and Séké inhabit the coastal region between Libreville and Cocobeach, near the border with Equatorial Guinea, in an area that they share with the predominant Fang. The remnants of the Ndiwa—arguably the first group to make contact with Europeans—were gradually absorbed by adjacent Mpongwé groups after the massacre by the Dutch in 1698.

The central region from the upper reaches of the Como River to the area west and south of the Woleu N'Tem is home to a number of ethnic groups of varying size and importance, mostly belonging to the Punu-Eshira linguistic group: the Okanda in the Ogooué-Ivindo basin; the Nzabi, who came from the Congo in the eighteenth century, in the N'gounié and Ogooué-Lolo; and the Bapounou, who reportedly came from Zaire, where they are known as Bayaka, in the seventeenth century, near the important regional towns of Mouila and Tchibanga. The Bapounou are closely allied linguistically and culturally with Eshira who inhabit the south-central region centering on the towns of Mandji and Fougamou.

The Bakota are divided geographically and culturally into two large groups: in the northeast, the Shamaye, Shake, Mahongoué, and Ndam-bomo make up one wing; in the south-central region around Lastoursville and Koulamoutu, several adjacent Mbété groups, notably the Obamba and Adouma, are allied culturally and linguistically with the Bakota. Like the Fang and the Myéné-speaking groups in the coastal regions, the Bakota represent an important dimension of Gabon's ethnic diversity. In the northeast, the Bakota are an important presence in the regional cities of Makokou and Mékambo near the iron ore deposits.[2] The Mékambo district is also home to some of Gabon's forest people, or Pygmies, who continue to live in relative isolation from others in the region. In 1962, French anthropologist Claude Cabrol reported a population of nearly 1,000 forest people in two major groups in the Mékambo cantons of Loué and Djoua. Small groups are also found in remote regions of the interior, particularly the N'Gounié and the Ogooué-Lolo. Gabon's total population of forest people is estimated at approximately 2,000.[3]

The Batéké are the Gabonese wing of an ethnic family centered in the neighboring Congo Republic. In fact, the Batéké territory was part of the Congo until 1922, when an adjustment of the internal borders of French Equatorial Africa assigned this section of the territory to Gabon.

The Gabonese Batéké are located near major uranium and manganese deposits in the southeastern region around Franceville, Gabon's third largest city. President Bongo is a Téké. In the central region, including the upper N'gounié and the area of the du Chaillu massif, the Mitsogho, Masango, and Apindji inhabit an area that remains isolated and remote from the major currents of Gabonese life. Travel from the distant interior regions to the coastal centers, Libreville and Port Gentil, is an arduous journey, and even today there is no way of reaching some areas of the country by road or rail; the important link between the political capital, Libreville, and the economic capital, Port Gentil, for example, must be accomplished by air or ocean travel.

Gabon's national borders are an artifact of European colonialism and events in Europe in the nineteenth and twentieth centuries that had important and lasting consequences for Africans. Gabon's current boundaries were determined by the terms of the peace after World War I and the reallocation of German colonies in Africa. As a result, ethnic groups like the Batéké and the Bakota found themselves included in a political structure with arbitrarily drawn borders unrelated to their traditional socioeconomic patterns. Ironically, French colonial efforts to exploit Gabon's abundant natural resources stimulated an awareness among Gabonese of the importance of different regions and the development of a common identity as members of the same polity. Due to their isolation from the peoples of the interior and their evolving identity with the foreign residents of the estuary, the Gabonese inhabitants of Libreville thought of themselves alone as the Gabonese, a tendency reinforced historically by the significance of the estuary.[4]

The pressures generated by the Europeans and their obsession with economic rewards brought about profound changes in traditional village life. Gabon was a society of villages without a central politico-economic core until the arrival of the Europeans and the designation of Libreville as the capital. Contact with Europeans and the installation of the French colonial apparatus forced fundamental changes in the pattern of relationships among the indigenous populations. Those ordained to power by kinship or birthright witnessed the shift of their authority to French administrators who ruled in the name of a new and physically powerful entity that the indigenous peoples, in all likelihood, would never see. In the time honored tradition of colonialism, the French exercised their acquired sovereignty by using persons in positions of traditional authority to maintain control over their subjects. A twentieth-century example of this practice was the appointment by the French, to further French interests, of the future president, Léon Mba, as *chef de canton* in Libreville's Fang district.

Village life, circa 1860 (photo courtesy of the Gabon National Archives).

The power and authority of the indigenous institutions diminished as individuals acquired new outlooks and radically different expectations about their futures. As the French influence increased and expanded throughout Gabon, hundreds of Gabonese received educations from French missionaries and accepted—in many cases reluctantly—the foreign culture. Life in the towns and cities epitomized the new style brought on by the transformation from subsistence agriculture and barter to the extractive, currency-based economy imposed by the French. Young Gabonese from different regions and ethnic groups moved to towns and cities to participate as wage earners in the new economy financed by timber, rubber, and, later, mining. Two very basic and important processes were simultaneously at work: the urbanization of the young and the transformation of peasant farmers into wage laborers. Although many remote villages changed little, the vast majority lost their most energetic members. The impact of colonial economic activities on the present disposition of the population is evident: Gabon's population today is distributed along the major axes of road and water transportation (see Figure 4.2). Without exception, the rural areas of the country are deserted in contrast to towns like Oyem, Ndjolé, Booué, and Mouila, whose growth reflects the penetration of the interior and the emergence of alternatives to subsistence agriculture—trading posts, logging camps, and uranium mines.[5]

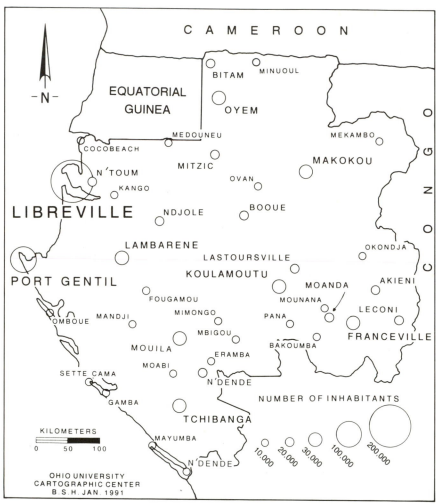

FIGURE 4.2 Urban Population

In this broad and still evolving context, the question of identity is a major one for the Gabonese. As in many areas of the world, there is a conflict in Gabon between ethnic and regional identities and the abstraction of the nation. Nationhood requires that diverse groups share some basic goals and aspirations. It was the French, in fact, who initiated the identity of the polity and formulated its political and economic agendas until independence, and even thereafter. Independence brought with it an expectation of universal participation, but the competition between the Fang and Myéné centered in Libreville was a major obstacle to the establishment of any sense of allegiance by those at a distance from the capital and alienated or unaffected by decisions made there, as PUNGA resentments in the preindependence era and recent Bapounou expressions of discontent illustrate. Nevertheless, a significant number of Gabonese appear to think of themselves in national terms and behave as if they belong to a common entity. Franceville, Port Gentil, Lambaréné, and other regional cities are now home to persons of diverse ethnic origins whose common experiences are often as important as their ethnic affiliations. Urbanization, with all of the stresses that accompany it, tends to under-mine parochial identities, and Gabon's urbanization has been relatively rapid. Libreville, for example, was a small town until independence; the population increased from 27,000 in 1960 to 175,000 in 1975 (see Figure 4.3). Similar changes took place in other cities and towns as the traditional peasant economy gave way to new occupations and forms of employment. The combined effect of these multiple influences is a national identity that is both recent and fragile.

RELIGION

The once-intense competition between Protestant and Catholic mis-sionaries ended in a Catholic victory, and many Gabonese continue a nominal affiliation to the Roman Catholic Church. According to official statistics, a slight majority of the Gabonese are Catholic; approximately 16 percent are of several Protestant denominations and the remainder are identified as "animists." It is important to note that the *gabonisation* of the church has produced mixed results; although the church hierarchy includes several bishops and an archbishop, Gabonese priests and nuns represent a minority of the personnel of the church. With respect to linguistic diversity, the practices of the church are more in tune with the ethnic reality than the official policies of the government. In Libreville, for example, masses are conducted in Fang by both French and Gabonese priests, and other regional languages are employed in services around the country. French remains the official national language, however, and is the language of instruction in the schools.

A highly publicized papal visit to Gabon in 1982 highlighted the Catholicism of the Gabonese. The Bongo government scrupulously cleaned the city of Libreville and constructed a new guest residence for the visiting entourage of church officials. With a display of national wealth, the government attempted to convince the visitors that Gabon was a pillar of Catholicism in black Africa. This was particularly ironic in light of Bongo's conversion to Islam in 1973 (although Bongo maintained that his conver-sion was a personal matter—and Islam is neither widespread nor appar-ently popular—observers noted at the time that the conversion coincided with an effort to secure Arab financial assistance).

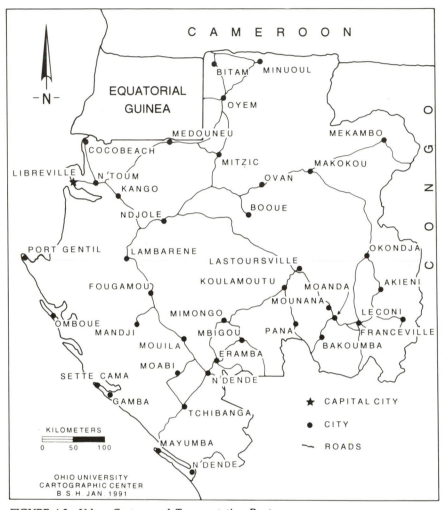

FIGURE 4.3   Urban Centers and Transportation Routes

Despite their attachment to Catholicism, many Gabonese continue to engage in rituals and practices based on traditions of animism that vary from forms of ancestor worship to secret male societies whose members believe in their power to transform themselves into lions or leopards. Within these rich traditions one finds a hierarchy of figures reputed to have the power to influence personal fortunes and political events. According to a number of observers, sorcerers play a significant role in contemporary Gabonese life. In 1984, the French Cultural Center in Libreville hosted an unusual public discussion of the role of sorcery in Gabon. Many prominent political figures, including President Bongo, are reported to consult with sorcerers on all major affairs of state; the most persistent rumor is that Bongo's marriage to Josephine Assele assured the good graces of his future mother-in-law, the most powerful of the Gabonese sorcerers. In his controversial book, *Affaires africaines*, Pierre Péan claimed that all the cabinet members in the Bongo government are expected to belong to a secret society, Ndjobi, that initiates new members in a ritual that requires them to drink water used to wash Bongo's feet. According to Péan, the ceremony takes place in the presence of Josephine Assele's father, who is reputed to possess special powers. Péan, and others, in an interesting variation on this theme, suggest that an important, secretive Masonic linkage exists as well among the Gabonese and French members of the *clan des gabonais*.[6]

In this context, it is important to note the complex and ambiguous role that women play in this world of magic and power in contemporary Gabon. Women have long been influential in clan affairs without holding formal positions, and the power of women sorcerers is an important component of the national folklore. Secret women's societies have rivaled the power and influence of their male counterparts, and many women have acquired positions of power and prestige in women's eyes and fear and respect from men who acknowledge a universe replete with rites and rituals that transform men and women into ferocious animals.[7] These segregated, secretive institutions reinforce traditions of male dominance, however; men do not share their secrets with women, and women fear reprisal for sharing their secrets with men.

The continuing power of sorcery in contemporary Gabon reinforces the perception that Gabon is a relatively young society only recently disengaged from a past in which animism was the predominant spiritual force. The concerted efforts of missionaries to carry Protestant and Catholic doctrines into the interior regions disrupted traditional religious patterns, turning some persons toward extreme and clandestine practices even as other traditional practices, such as the selling of amulets by street vendors to ward off illness or misfortune, were trivialized. The observant visitor to the Mont Bouët central market in Libreville will witness a steady stream of purchases of the various ingredients needed to make potions to protect against enemies or obtain good fortune. A widespread belief in magic persists in various forms throughout the society, apparently irrespective of education, family background, or social class. Visitors in search of trinkets and souvenirs may not sense the nearness of this vast reservoir of energy to the surface of Gabonese life.

At a more institutionalized level, the phenomenon known as Bwiti deserves special attention. Bwiti is referred to by anthropologists as a syncretic religion, that is, one that brings together elements of indigenous beliefs with those imposed by the outsiders. In its ritual and cosmology,

Bwiti combines the animist heritage of precolonial Gabon with the form and structure of Roman Catholicism. Bwiti's power is a result of its syncretic character, the union of traditional Fang rituals and beliefs with the radically different worldview promulgated by those who conquered the country. In their separate studies on Bwiti and the Fang, Georges Balandier and James Fernandez explained that syncretic religions like Bwiti allow traditional societies to cope with the discontinuity and disruption that accompanies colonialism.[8] Mademoiselle, an antiwitchcraft movement of the 1940s, was another expression of Fang preoccupation with the pace and scope of change in their communities.

Bwiti ceremonies incorporate elements of a Catholic mass, although the use of the hallucinegenic drug *iboga* to induce trances in which one seeks communion with one's ancestors is clearly not an acceptable practice for the conventional Catholic. Throughout the period of French administration, Bwiti was illegal and considered sacrilegious. The sect reportedly originated as a secret male society among the Mitsogho in the remote region of the du Chaillu massif and spread to intruding Fang clans in the nineteenth century. Bwiti is widely practiced in the Fang regions of Gabon and, after independence until very recently, was tolerated by the authorities.

In 1987, suspecting that some religious groups harbored political dissidents, the government banned a number of them, following a meeting between Bongo and the leaders of the Catholic and Protestant communities and the small Moslem population. This action against the sects followed accusations of ritualistic murders by Bwiti members (the suspicion that Bwiti adherents engage in ritualistic human sacrifices also received considerable attention during the Léon Mba incident in 1933). The ban against sects applies also to the Témoins de Jehova (Jehovah's Witnesses), who have engaged in evangelical activities in several areas of the country. In banning these groups, the government seems sensitive to organizations that might form a core of political opposition under the guise of religious activities—the execution of Captain Alexandre Ngokouta in 1985 is a case in point—and Bongo appears to be particularly concerned about dissident groups in Fang communities. It is quite likely, however, that the ban against these various groups will be lifted in light of what some commentators are referring to as Bongostroika.

CLASS, STRATIFICATION, AND ETHNICITY

The Gabonese sociologist Laurent Biffot observed that literacy is the most significant factor in the transition from "traditional" to "modern" societies. An obvious, but often overlooked, point is that this ability to

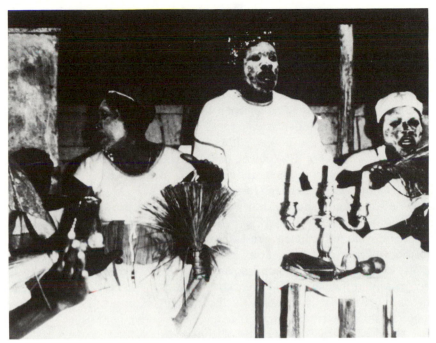

Bwiti ceremony of the Renzi rite (photo courtesy of the Gabon National Archives).

read and write is in the language of the colonial power. Gabon shares an experience common to many former colonies: the lack of any single politically acceptable indigenous language and continuing reliance on the language of the European colonizers as the medium of national communication.

During the colonial era, a hierarchy of relationships developed between the French and the Gabonese and among the various indigenous Gabonese based on levels of competence in the French language and acceptance of the legitimacy of the foreign presence. Status in Gabon continues to reflect this historical relationship. The current Gabonese elite manage an array of institutions that they have carried over from the colonial regime, and literacy in French continues to be one of the criteria for social, political, and economic success. In this context, the extensive and persistent French presence in the country has special significance to the very idea of social class in Gabon. To understand the significance of social class in Gabon means to acknowledge the extent to which political and economic power is in the hands of the French and those members of the Gabonese elite involved in the affairs of the economy and the state.

Biffot's work is significant in its focus on a critical dimension of power in contemporary Gabon. In discussing the class structure of Gabonese society, Biffot explained that contemporary Gabon—and all former colonies—consists of three major classes: (1) the holders of power, (2) those who control the wealth or means of production, and (3) subalterns, that is, those whose labor is used for the production of material goods. He distinguished those who acceded to the formal reins of power upon the granting of independence from those, almost exclusively non-nationals, who exercised economic power. Although susceptible to the challenge that economic power is political power, Biffot's analysis illuminates a reality of Gabonese politics crucial to understanding the current policies of the Bongo regime.[9] Control of the formal institutions of government does not automatically confer power, but such control does provide a crucial opportunity to bargain with those who have preeminent interests in the economic system. In the case of Gabon, the French are in a commanding position with respect to an array of decisions affecting the economic life of the country. To understand social class in this context is simply to recognize that the very structure of the ruling system contains a presence that is not necessarily attuned to the interests of either the indigenous peoples or those who rule in their name. Used correctly, class is a concept that should illustrate the reality of the distribution of power and the distribution of the nation's wealth.

It is well known that the per capita income of the Gabonese is among the highest in Africa. What is much less certain is the distribution of the nation's wealth to those who make up Biffot's subaltern class, that is, the Gabonese on the economic fringes and the expatriate Africans who have been recruited to supplement the meager numbers of Gabonese in the work force. It is a common refrain that there is no poverty in Gabon, and in contrast to the abject conditions that one encounters in other areas of the continent, at first glance Gabon does appear to be an African paradise. But, as noted in Chapter 3, poverty does exist, suffered by the lowest strata of the subaltern class in glaring contrast to the conspicuous consumption of those nationals and expatriates who control the nation's wealth. Gabon's extensive reliance on foreign workers and the disparity in wage levels between Gabonese and non-Gabonese African workers is one dimension of a complex class-strata system that allocates economic rewards on the basis of residence and citizenship. Recently, the number of non-Gabonese Africans working in the country was estimated at 200,000; if one assumes a Gabonese population of approximately 950,000, non-Gabonese African workers represent more than 20 percent of the population—a substantial proportion. The French population may have been as high as 30,000 in the 1970s, with a decline to approximately 18,000 reported in the past decade. One might expect, however, that those remaining French nationals fulfill very critical roles in the Gabonese economic system. As recently as 1980, 81 percent of the positions in the private sector classified as *cadres et techniciens supérieurs* (managerial and advanced technical) were held by French nationals; in marked contrast, 80 percent of the positions in the private sector requiring minimal qualifications were held by Gabonese. In the category of *main-d'oeuvre banale* (common labor), 17 percent of the positions were held by non-Gabonese Africans. Since 1970, recurring periods of austerity have clearly exacerbated tensions between the various strata and raised important questions about the judgment and management skills of the governing class.[10]

The political and economic life of the country is visibly marked by allegiances and obligations based on ethnicity that determine the manner in which individuals interact with each other. Obligation to family and clan demands that the newly arrived relative receive consideration for a position in the office or factory regardless of official merit and performance criteria. In a society that is exhorted to work and sacrifice for the common good, the obligations of ethnicity and kinship clash with and in some cases undermine expectations of competence and efficiency. The expectations of those still linked to the rural kinship system are difficult to satisfy in an environment that lays primary emphasis on production and profit.

The issue of ethnicity is intimately related to President Bongo's political power. As an outsider to the bitter contest for power among the Fang and Myéné, Bongo's accession to the presidency represented, in his view and that of his supporters, a possibility for a consensus based on national unity. Ethnicity remains, however, a decisive factor in the reality of political and economic relationships in Gabon. Bongo maintains a consistent policy of representing Gabon's major ethnic groups (and his minority Batéké group) in influential positions. His long political success is based on a masterful sense of balance reinforced by promises of substantial prestige and material rewards to those who express their allegiance to the regime. He is also adept at the more unsavory practice of using the substantial foreign presence to promote Gabonese nationalism, a technique that has produced periods of intense xenophobia, including physical attacks on Gabon's large and diverse expatriate population.

EDUCATION

Gabon has one of the highest literacy rates in Africa, estimated in 1985 at nearly 70 percent. In the postindependence era, the government successfully developed a national school system that enrolls nearly all eligible students. In 1986, approximately 173,000 students were enrolled in 929 primary schools—558 public, 247 Catholic, and 124 of Protestant denominations. Institutions of secondary education enroll nearly 25,000

Primary school students marching in the annual parade celebrating the founding of the PDG (photo by the author).

students in approximately 45 public and parochial institutions. Additionally, nearly 5,000 students are enrolled in schools providing a technical curriculum.[11] In Libreville, the elite lycée Léon Mba and several primary and secondary schools that accept significant numbers of French students find their teaching ranks supplemented by a corps of French *coopérants*, who are engaged to make the schools competitive with those in France. This is of particular importance to the French and the Gabonese elite who expect their offspring to continue their education in France.

Teacher education forms a significant national effort to provide Gabonese teachers for both public and parochial education. Nearly 4,000 students are enrolled in 23 institutions training teachers for instruction in the primary and secondary schools. At the pinnacle of the system is the Université Omar Bongo (UOB) and, in the French manner, a network of *grandes écoles*. In addition to UOB, Libreville is the site of seven *grandes écoles*, the most notable being the Ecole nationale d'administration, the Ecole nationale de la magistrature, and for the training of teachers, the Ecole normale supérieure. In 1986, there were slightly more than 4,000 students enrolled in university and professional programs and more than 1,000 Gabonese in institutions outside of Gabon, the largest number in France and Morocco, but a growing number going to the United States and Canada (Bongo's two daughters studied for a time at UCLA).[12] In the classical disciplines, literature, law, and so forth, most students pursue their advanced studies in France. The young Gabonese studying outside of the country pose a continuing problem of a "brain drain"—students wishing to remain in the places where they establish professional and social contacts. The acute problem is exacerbated by the absence in Gabon of career opportunities for many of the returning foreign-trained professionals. Periods of austerity and the financial commitment to complete the Transgabonais limit the capacity of the government to create positions for this important group.

The government has cut back on grants for study abroad. In 1984, there was an initial reduction of almost 400 *bourses* (scholarships)—from 1,506 to 1,109, a decision reflecting the general tightening of the purse strings as well as acknowledging the major problem in absorbing returning graduates into the local economy. It has been the long-standing practice of the government to use the national bureaucracy as a safety valve to hire large numbers of graduates who would otherwise be unemployed, resulting in a disproportionately large corps of civil servants. Between 1970 and 1980, for example, the percentage of *cadres et techniciens supérieurs* in the public sector more than doubled, although a similar classification of employees in the private sector experienced a slight decline.[13] The decrease in the number of supported students studying abroad represents a general reduction in the percentage of students receiving financial support in the past decade—a drop from 87 to 77 percent—a result of government concern that it is compounding its problems by supporting students in areas that are least likely to contribute to the development of the economy. One suspects also that opposition to the Bongo regime on the part of a number of students and expatriates in France may affect the government's attitude about study in foreign places.

In organization and content, the educational system is decidedly French. Instruction is given in French, and the seven-year cycle that constitutes the initial educational phase leads to the classical French *baccalaureat* or the more technically oriented *brévét du premier cycle*. Since 1970, the government has intensified efforts to channel students into technical areas more suited to the economic requirements of the country.

Religious schools continue to play a part in the education of Gabon's youth. Both Catholic and Protestant schools receive subsidies from the government, and the combined number of Catholic and Protestant institutions represent nearly 30 percent of the schools involved in primary education. In Libreville, students in Catholic and Protestant schools represent slightly less than 30 percent of the total primary school population, but the proportion is considerably higher in the Woleu N'Tem, where the Catholic population makes up more than 50 percent of the total number of students receiving primary instruction. It is noteworthy, as well, that the Woleu N'Tem has the largest number of students enrolled in Protestant schools in the country.[14] This is probably due to the displacement in the late nineteenth century of many Protestant missionaries from the estuary to the north of the country.

Although Gabon's national contribution to education is substantial, countries with markedly fewer national resources are more generous in their support of education. In 1985, the neighboring Congo Republic, for example, spent 6 percent of GNP on education; the Gabonese spent only 4.6 percent of GNP. The Central African Republic, certainly one of the poorest of the African states, spent 4.9 percent of GNP that same year.[15] It is also apparent that the Bongo regime has a particularly limited view of the role of higher education. Library facilities at UOB, for example, are virtually nonexistent, and inadequate food service and sanitary facilities on the campus were implicated in the student unrest of 1990.

Education is an area of tension between French and Gabonese. French professors, although declining in numbers, remain in positions throughout the Gabonese educational hierarchy despite *gabonisation*. At UOB, only half of the members of the faculty are Gabonese. The remaining half are not all French—they include Haitians, Martiniquans, and others— but the low proportion of Gabonese represents a major problem of identity and sovereignty both for the Gabonese government and for a number of the Gabonese faculty and students, who complain bitterly of this remaining symbol of French imperialism.

The creation of the Centre universitaire de science politique et de développement (CUSPOD) illustrates another element of tension in current Gabonese higher education. CUSPOD began as a training school for cadres of the governing PDG. In the early 1980s, CUSPOD received authorization from the government to grant university degrees in direct competition with UOB. Under the budgetary austerity of the mid-1980s and continuing pressure from the UOB administration, CUSPOD's academic career was ended. CUSPOD's existence both challenged UOB's monopoly on academic credentials and called attention to the increased value of university credentials in the Gabonese employment market.

PUBLIC HEALTH

Gabon's success in developing a literate, educated population is not matched in the critical area of public health, in which serious problems continue to undermine efforts at national economic development.

Gabon's relatively small population is a direct consequence of a high rate of infant mortality and a high infertility rate among women of childbearing years (ages 15 to 49). In 1986, United Nations sources reported an infant mortality rate of 229 deaths per 1,000 births—the highest rate of mortality reported on the continent, although challenged by Gabonese officials. A more accurate figure, according to statisticians at

UOB, is 150 deaths per 1,000 births. The exact figures may be uncertain, but the reality is that a relatively low birthrate is one dimension of Gabon's modest population size.[16]

Infant mortality is directly related to the quality of both prenatal and postnatal care, to which the distribution of the population and the concentration of public health infrastructure in the estuary region contribute. Over 60 percent of the doctors and surgeons in the country live and practice in the Libreville region; one finds here, as well, the largest concentration of medical facilities. Only 25 percent of the Gabonese live in the region of the estuary, however. In an even closer link to infant mortality, all the gynecologists practicing in the country in 1980 were in Libreville.[17]

Infertility is a common problem in central Africa. Gabon appears to share with other areas of equatorial Africa a generalized epidemic, affecting men and women, and derived from complex strains of venereal diseases that have affected these populations for several centuries. Although no resolution of the problem seems imminent, research is under way in Franceville at the Centre international de récherches médicales. Funded by Elf Gabon and the Gabonese government, medical research devoted to the problem of infertility was supplemented in 1987 by research on the AIDS virus. In 1990, in an unprecedented admission of a serious public health concern, the government, with the financial assistance of the French Ministry of Cooperation, sponsored a major anti-AIDS information campaign throughout the country. Although there are no authoritative figures on the number of AIDS cases in Gabon, estimates vary from 6 to 10 percent of the population. In comparison, estimates of the incidence of AIDS in Ivory Coast and neighboring Cameroon are somewhat higher.[18]

With the exception of the AIDS virus and the persistent problem of infertility, the health of the Gabonese has significantly improved. Epidemics of yellow fever and smallpox have been eliminated by aggressive public health campaigns in most of the countries of central Africa. Malaria remains fairly common among the indigenous population, but the overall incidence of the disease has declined.

Any discussion of health care in Gabon would be incomplete without mention of the hospital founded in 1924 by Albert Schweitzer in Lambaréné on the Ogooué River. Known throughout the world, the hospital continues to attract an impressive number of foreign visitors. Today it is operated by an international medical team supported by the Schweitzer Foundation and, since 1977, the Gabonese government. Schweitzer, who died in 1965, came to Gabon in 1912 as a medical missionary sponsored by the Société des missions évangélique de Paris (SMF). He and his wife worked in Lambaréné until World War I, when the French authorities raised questions about their loyalty. (The Schweitzers had come from

Cross marking the grave of Dr. Albert Schweitzer in Lambaréné
(photo by the author).

Alsace, one of the two French provinces annexed by Germany following
the Franco-German War of 1871.) They were interned in France until the
end of the war, but returned to Gabon in 1924 and established the present
hospital near the site of the original SME mission.

Schweitzer raised controversy with his abandonment of traditional
European notions of hygiene and patient care in deference to climate and
indigenous social practices. The hospital grounds at Lambaréné were
crowded with relatives of patients, who assisted in their care and support.

Although Schweitzer found support for his unorthodox medical practices, more serious criticisms were reserved for his alleged racist views about Africans. Albert Schweitzer's work on a small island in the Ogooué River will continue to be a controversial part of an important era of Gabon's history.[19]

COMMUNICATIONS

The pattern of communications in Gabon reflects the political and economic development of the country as a French colony. Libreville is the center of a network of newspaper, radio, and television services that transmit the views of the government throughout the country. Until the liberalization that began in 1990, there was only one daily newspaper—the government-owned and -published, *L'Union*. Although it has a circulation estimated at only 15,000, *L'Union* is closely followed because of its role as the voice of the Bongo government. In its editorials and coverage of both domestic and international events, *L'Union* is decidedly noncontroversial and a faithful expression of the policies of the Bongo regime; even the irreverent Makaya does not transcend these limits.

All of the major French newspapers, newsmagazines, and journals of opinion (and the *International Herald Tribune, Time,* and *Newsweek*) are regularly available in the two largest population centers, Libreville and Port Gentil. Distribution to the provincial areas, including the administrative centers, is often interrupted by the rainy seasons as well as the eternal Gabonese problem of access to some of the more remote areas of the country. New local newspapers are now appearing, associated with the various parties and factions that have emerged since the Democracy conference. There are, as well, several specialized publications; the most notable, *Le Patriote*, a satirical magazine modeled on *Le Canard enchaîné*, the Parisian weekly, was banned during the disturbances that took place following Joseph Rendjame's death in Libreville in May 1990. *Dialogue*, the official publication of the PDG, has limited circulation.

Radio and television represent the most extensive efforts to establish an effective means of national communications, and both are used to disseminate a wide range of information about domestic and international events. Radio Gabon, known as the Voice of Renovation, broadcasts daily from Libreville with a standard format including popular music, cultural activities, and news reports. Radio Gabon is the official voice of the government, and its newscasts and comments on events in Gabon or in the world faithfully reflect the views of the government. More ambitious is Radio-Télévision Gabon (RTG), which operates a national channel as well as a second channel exclusively for the Libreville region. For its national broadcasts, RTG transmits from stations in Libreville, Port Gentil,

and Franceville; a system of relay stations distributes the signals throughout the country. RTG's second channel broadcasts from the presidential
palace in Libreville. Although the content of the Libreville channel does
not differ significantly from that of the national broadcasts, its very location
in the heavily guarded presidential compound insures the government's
ability to control information during a crisis.

Both radio and television are routinely used to disseminate the views
of the president on a wide range of subjects. A Gabonese version of fireside
chats with President Bongo is a standard feature of both radio and
television, providing frequent opportunities for the president to take his
message to the Gabonese people. The extent to which that message reaches
beyond Libreville, however, is an important question. A UN census of
radio and television ownership in 1987 found 100 radios and 20 television
sets per thousand population.[20] If, as seems likely, the greater number of
these receivers are owned by the more affluent residents of Libreville, Port
Gentil, and Franceville, the message may be restricted to those already
associated intimately with the regime as part of the elite structure.

In a significant departure from historic practice, the government
agreed to the installation of private cable television channels in 1987 and
1988. Télé-Africa, funded by Gabonese and Swiss capital, began trans-
missions in 1987, followed by programs provided by the French cable
firm, Canal plus Afrique, a subsidiary of the French television network,
Antenne 2, in 1988. Africa Number 1 is a commercial radio station jointly
owned by the Gabonese government and a consortium of French investors.
Broadcasting since 1981, Number 1 employs a fast-paced U.S. disk jockey
style with an extensive repertoire of popular west African music and the
releases of major black U.S. performers. With new transmission facilities
recently installed, Number 1 is heard throughout francophone Africa; it
initiated English-language broadcasts several years ago. Its success as a
popular regional station should not obscure the fact that its broadcasts are
susceptible to the same stringent censorship applied to the government
media. The Péan affair in 1983 made it dramatically clear that Gabon's
total communications network is directly and tightly controlled by President Bongo.[21]

NOTES

1. Quoted in Georges Balandier, *Sociologie actuelle de l'Afrique noire: Dynamique sociale en Afrique central* (Paris: Quadrige/Presses universitaire de France,
1982), p. 73; translation by the author.
2. For a detailed description of Gabon's ethnic groups, see Ange Ratanga-
Atoz, *Initiation à l'histoire générale du Gabon* (Libreville: Ministère de l'éducation
nationale/Université Omar Bongo, 1979), pp. 60–84; for current spatial-demo-

graphic data on Gabon's ethnic groups, see Ministère de l'éducation nationale de la république gabonaise, *Géographie et cartographie du Gabon* (Paris: Editions classique d'expression française, 1981), pp. 22–25.

3. Claude Cabrol, *Notes sur les pygmées de Mekambo*, Mimeo, Gabon National Library, 1962.

4. The seminal work on Gabonese nationalism is Brian Weinstein, *Nation-Building on the Ogooué* (Cambridge, Mass.: Harvard University Press, 1966).

5. For a graphic depiction of the population, see Ministère de l'éducation, *Géographie et Cartographie du Gabon*, pp. 48–51.

6. Pierre Péan, *Affaires africaines* (Paris: Fayard, 1983), pp. 32–36. For a study of magic and the occult in Gabon, see André Raponda-Walker and Roger Sillans, *Rites et croyances des peuples du Gabon* (Paris: Présence Africaine, 1962), especially Part 3, Chapters 1–3.

7. Raponda-Walker and Sillans, *Rites et croyances des peuple du Gabon*, Chapters 1–3.

8. Balandier, *Sociologie actuelle de l'Afrique noire*, Chapter 2; and James Fernandez, *Bwiti: An Ethnography of the Religious Imagination in Africa* (Princeton, N.J.: Princeton University Press, 1982). The analysis in Part 1 is particularly helpful in understanding the manner in which the Fang have attempted to manage change.

9. Laurent Biffot, "Genèse des classes sociales au Gabon," *Annales de l'école nationale d'administration* (Libreville), 2 (1977), pp. 33–48.

10. International Labour Organization, *L'emploi et répartition des revenus dans la république gabonaise* (Addis Ababa: International Labour Office, 1984), pp. 24–28.

11. United Nations, *Statistical Yearbook, 1987*, pp. 216–244.

12. Ibid., p. 181.

13. International Labour Organization, *L'emploi et répartition des revenus dans la république gabonaise*, pp. 26–28.

14. Ministère de l'éducation, *Géographie et cartographie du Gabon*, pp. 100–105.

15. United Nations, *Statistical Yearbook, 1987*, p. 245.

16. Ibid., pp. 64–65.

17. Ministère de l'éducation, *Géographie et cartographie du Gabon*, pp. 107–110.

18. Ariane Poissonier, "Faites l'amour et pas la mort," *Jeune Afrique*, no. 1561 (November 28–December 4, 1990), pp. 36–37.

19. For a critical examination of Schweitzer's role in Gabon, see Moïse Nkoghve-Mve, "le Docteur Schweitzer et la colonisation," *Réalités gabonaises*, January–February 1977, pp. 21–26. Additionally, Schweitzer's notebooks provide interesting insights into his work and his perceptions about his patients and their lives; see Albert Schweitzer, *From My African Notebook* (London: Allen and Unwin, 1938) and *More From the Primeval Forest* (London: Allen and Unwin, 1931).

20. United Nations, *Statistical Yearbook, 1987*.

21. For an account of the blackout, see Nicole Guez, "Gabon-France: La méprise," *Jeune Afrique économie*, no. 28 (December 8, 1983), pp. 15–18.

5

Foreign Relations

During Léon Mba's presidency, Gabon's presence in the constellation of newly independent African nations was hardly noticed. As one of the smallest former colonies and the one perhaps most effectively limited by its political and psychological links to France, Gabon, on gaining independence, did not precipitate an effort to change the course of the direction set during the period of French colonization. Mba was preoccupied with consolidating his internal political control. The exercise and direction of foreign policy was limited by both his political agenda and the constraints of the cooperation accords of 1960, by which Gabon was obligated to accept French review of its foreign policy. Mba's death and Bongo's accession to the presidency introduced an era characterized by efforts to expand Gabon's African and international role and, correspondingly reduce its extensive economic dependency on France. Gabon's ties with France do, however, explain its general outlook on African and world affairs. Gabon's foreign policy reflects a Gaullist antipathy toward regional or international pacts or agreements that limit or constrain national sovereignty.

In the pattern of his predecessor, Bongo's first priority was the institutionalization of the one-party state. The founding of the PDG and its subsequent elevation to constitutional status gave Bongo the internal support required to build the foundation for a postpetroleum economy and, specifically in that context, to fulfill his pledge to build the Transgabonais railway. Throughout Bongo's tenure as president, Gabon's foreign policy has reflected the pursuit of economic goals.

FRANCE AND GABON

Gabon's special relationship with France remains intact despite occasional moments of tension and disagreement. In 1974, in an effort to reduce the influence of the French in its affairs, Gabon negotiated new political and financial terms with France, ending French review of Gabon's

foreign policy and France's exclusive right to Gabon's uranium. To eliminate a troubling symbol of the colonial era, French citizens no longer
qualified automatically for Gabonese citizenship.

Despite these changes, until the election of François Mitterrand as
president of France in 1981, bilateral relations were relatively uneventful.
Georges Pompidou's succession to the presidency after de Gaulle's death
in 1970 did not lead to any changes in the relationship, and Bongo
maintained a close personal friendship with Pompidou's successor, Valéry
Giscard d'Estaing. In the Mitterrand-Giscard presidential contest in 1981,
Bongo contributed heavily to Giscard's presidential campaign and went
on record as a critic of Mitterrand and his Socialist agenda. Bongo was
not very popular in Socialist circles, and MORENA became the vehicle
for Gabonese influence within the French Socialist party after its victory
in the French parliamentary elections of 1981. Several incidents in 1982
and 1983 culminated in the most significant confrontation between the
two governments since Gabon's independence.

The first incident involved the publication of Pierre Péan's *Affaires
africaines*. Péan's allegations of Bongo's complicity in a long string of
abuses, including assassinations, created a storm in Paris and a virtual
earthquake in Libreville. The publication of *Affaires africaines* was followed
by a televised MORENA press conference that rubbed additional salt in
Bongo's wounds. These events took place in a climate that the Bongo
regime regarded as increasingly prejudicial. In 1982, the broadcast by the
French television network, Antenne 2, of a documentary film, *Soleil voilé*
(The Veiled Sun), undermined efforts to improve Gabon's image in France.
A joint venture of Antenne 2 and the Gabonese government, the film was
intended to form an important part of a public relations campaign to
demonstrate the positive accomplishments of the Bongo government to
the French people. Without the knowledge of the Gabonese, however, the
final version of the documentary included an interview with the MORENA
leader Paul Mba Abessole. In the interview, Abessole recounted MOR-
ENA's charges against the Bongo regime and recalled the government's
poor record of respecting human rights. In 1982, MORENA had received
extensive coverage in the Parisian press during the trial of MORENA
members in the alleged plot to overthrow Bongo.[1]

It was at the time of the publication of *Affaires africaines*, and the
attendant publicity, that Bongo ordered the curious blackout of news about
France in the Gabonese media. For some time Bongo had perceived threats
from within Gabon and now, for the first time, he confronted a government
in Paris that appeared to sympathize with MORENA and other critics of
the regime who had for many years called on the French government to
limit the excesses of the Bongo government. The manner in which this
series of events was concluded by the two governments is revealing.

Following Bongo's blackout decision, Mitterrand dispatched several special emissaries to Libreville, culminating with Prime Minister Pierre Mauroy, in a highly publicized visit in March 1984. During his visit to Libreville, Mauroy attempted also to calm the French expatriate community, which feared that Péan's attack on Bongo could lead to the harassment or expulsion of French nationals. Mauroy's task was made more difficult by the hostility of many in the French community toward the Mitterrand regime—the overseas vote in the presidential and legislative elections of 1981 had been decidedly in favor of Giscard and antagonistic toward Mitterrand and the Socialists.

The French realized—and Bongo capitalized on this fact—that Gabon was increasingly restive and that Bongo's decision to open the door to a number of U.S. petroleum and mining firms could jeopardize France's access to Gabon's strategic resources; the French ended with inviting Bongo to make a state visit to France and acceded to his request for a small nuclear reactor and a promise to limit the activities and public exposure of MORENA in France. This promise was accompanied by an unconvincing reminder to the Gabonese that France was a country that respected freedom of the press and that the French government would not practice censorship. In 1985, in a revealing footnote to the affair, Jean-Christophe Mitterrand, the president's son and adviser on African affairs, accepted an appointment to the board of the manganese firm COMILOG. Both *père et fils* denied any impropriety in the appointment.[2]

In the French presidential election of May 1988, Bongo indicated his preference for the candidacy of Jacques Chirac, although it was reported that Bongo hedged his bets by also contributing to Mitterrand's campaign, as well as that of the extreme right-wing candidate, Jean-Marie Le Pen, who had included a trip to Gabon in his 1987 campaign. Bongo did refuse the request from some French residents to establish a Gabon section of Le Pen's Front national, but in supplying funds to Le Pen's organization, Bongo supported a group that is decidedly racist, anti-immigrant, and xenophobic.

During the period of *cohabitation* between Mitterrand and Chirac following the defeat of the Socialists in the parliamentary elections of 1986, relations between Bongo and the Chirac majority in the French National Assembly were cordial. The victory of the Socialists in the parliamentary elections of 1988 and Michel Rocard's appointment as prime minister renewed the possibility for friction between the two governments. It is more likely, however, that the Mitterrand, or, for that matter, any French government, will tread lightly in its dealings with the Bongo government. Both Mitterrand and Rocard have denied that sending the Foreign Legion to Port Gentil to "protect French nationals" could be interpreted as support for the Bongo regime.[3] The decision to send French troops clearly underlined the fact that France has no apparent intention of jeopardizing its economic and strategic investments in Gabon. Mitterrand's pledge not to interfere in Gabon's internal affairs must be understood as a calculated preference for Bongo and the status quo over the unknown.

One can only conclude that the special relationship continues. Despite Bongo's skill at creating uncertainty in Paris, Gabon remains a strong ally, a point that Bongo reiterated during his triumphant visit to France in 1984. Bongo counts on French military and economic support, although France's refusal to come to Hamani Diori's rescue following a military coup d'état in Niger in 1974 apparently worried Bongo. It is certain that the French have a strong interest in maintaining solid relations with Gabon. The unknown factor is the extent to which a growing number of Gabonese resent French influence and whether more nationalistic attitudes will prevail. It is quite likely, however, that Gabon's preoccupation with its new internal political agenda will preclude any fundamental changes in its relationship with France in the near future.

INTER-AFRICAN RELATIONS

Gabon's relations with other African nations are best described as tumultuous. Gabon was one of four African countries to pledge support to the Biafran secessionists, and Bongo's name was linked with mercenary efforts to overthrow the governments of Benin and the Congo Republic. There are, as well, numerous reports of collaboration with the former Smith regime in Rhodesia and the South African government during the Botha era.

Gabonese support for Biafra was not a surprise; de Gaulle was a vocal supporter of the Biafran secession, and the decision of the Gabonese to support Biafra bears the imprint of France in the conduct of Gabon's foreign affairs. In defense of Gabon's actions, Bongo stated that he could not quietly accept the "pogrom" instituted by the Nigerian government against 14 million Biafrans. More than 4,000 Biafran children were evacuated to Libreville, and many remained there even after the conclusion of the war in 1970. Nigeria charged that foreign mercenaries received regular shipments of supplies from an airlift originating at the Léon Mba airport in Libreville. Despite Bongo's denial of Gabonese assistance, it was well known at the time that Gabon was on the side of the Biafrans. Later, Gabon normalized its relationship with Nigeria, restoring formal diplomatic relations in 1973.

On more than one occasion, Bongo stated that he would make an alliance with the devil if necessary to secure financial assistance for the construction of the Transgabonais. Although South African assistance in financing the Transgabonais did not materialize, negotiations between the two governments did take place; the Bongo government was ultimately unwilling to risk the condemnation that would have followed an agreement. There are unconfirmed reports, however, that Gabon did receive funds from an international consortium that may have been an intermediary for the South Africans.

Bongo plays an independent role in his conduct of foreign affairs, as is most apparent in Gabon's relationships with other African countries and the Organization for African Unity (OAU). Bongo professes adherence to the goals of the OAU even as he works to undermine the embargo on trade with South Africa, and for many years, Gabon engaged in clandestine trade with Rhodesia, including the exchange of Rhodesian beef and vegetables for Gabonese plywood.[4] Bongo also attempts to exert a leadership role in the OAU and is often hard pressed to explain inconsistencies in Gabon's dealings with its fellow African countries. Tension surfaced, for example, in 1978 at the OAU conference in Khartoum when the government of Benin accused Gabon of collusion in an effort to overthrow the Kerekou government. Bongo simply denied Gabonese collusion and ordered the expulsion of nearly 10,000 Beninois from the country.

In defending trade with South Africa, Bongo cites Houphouët-Boigny's argument for dialogue with the South Africans. The difference between dialogue and trade seems obvious, but the exchange benefited the two countries and Bongo is, if nothing else, a devoted pragmatist. In Angola, for example, Bongo on different occasions sided with both parties to the dispute, even applauding the Cuban presence that he initially condemned. But he also receives occasional praise for his actions in support of African liberation. Gabon hosted the exile government of São Tomé and Príncipe for a number of years, and Bongo was an active participant in the resolution of Chad's war with Libya. It is quite likely that his conversion to Islam and preexisting relationship with Libya facilitated his role as an intermediary in the dispute.

For many years, non-Gabonese African workers—Cameroonians, Congolese, Beninois and Equatorial Guineans—have supplemented the relatively small Gabonese work force; Gabon also has agreements with Burundi and the Central African Republic for contract workers in the mining areas of the country. On several occasions, the presence of these non-Gabonese workers has severely strained relationships between Gabon and the workers' countries of origin. The Gabonese often charge the workers with fomenting dissension, and friction is continual between Gabonese and foreigners over the Gabonese perception that the foreign share of the salaries and wages in the Gabonese economy is too substantial. Although the foreign presence is both large and noticeable, the Gabonese economy could not function without the expanded work force.

The Gabonese do not, however, accept this state of affairs gracefully, and the government occasionally sanctions reprisals against foreigners. In 1962, the Gabonese government expelled a number of Congolese workers following a disputed soccer match in Brazzaville, and the government gave tacit approval to attacks on residents of the Congolese neighborhoods in Libreville. Bongo's marriage in 1989 to the daughter of Congolese President Denis Sassou-Nguesso represents an important improvement in Gabon-Congo relations after years of old grievances and intermittent conflict.

Skirmishes between fishermen from Gabon and Equatorial Guinea provoked a dispute over national borders and fishing rights and the expulsion of thousands of Equatorial Guineans from Gabon. Accusations that followers of Paul Biya in Cameroon plotted to overthrow the Gabonese government strained relations between the two governments, and a soccer match in Douala in 1981 sparked a conflict between Gabon and Cameroon that involved attacks on Cameroonians in Gabon and the subsequent expulsion of thousands of Cameroonian workers. Although these conflicts were resolved and relatively cordial relations appear now to exist between the governments, the image of a xenophobic Gabon remains as a legacy of the incidents. Most recently, Gabon and Cameroon clashed over a Gabonese initiative to install a post of the national police on the Cameroonian side of the border to control the large numbers of Cameroonian workers who enter Gabon without documentation.

Recent physical attacks on Lebanese merchants illustrate the government's penchant for finding scapegoats in the expatriate community. Immigrants from a number of countries—Lebanese, Malians, Senegalese—have replaced the French and the few Gabonese who operated small retail and wholesale businesses. In 1986, the government instructed the residents of Libreville to harass such merchants, who were, according to Bongo, ruining the economy. At the same time, Bongo claimed that the morality of the capital city was endangered by foreign prostitutes, and he directed the police and the citizenry to take direct action against them. In the same year, the government announced its intention to implement a high-technology immigrant control system employing computer terminals at all airports and police stations. Gabon is particularly sensitive to the ease with which Equatorial Guineans and Cameroonians enter the country without proper documentation. That many of the illegal immigrants from these two countries are Fang creates an added concern for the Gabonese authorities.[5]

Although Gabon's political relationships with its most immediate neighbors have been erratic and often hostile, Gabon has been a reliable partner in the economic sphere. Gabon is a founding member and active participant of the Union douanière et économique de l'Afrique centrale

(UDEAC), which provides the Gabonese with immediate economic benefits. The other member states are neighboring Cameroon, Chad, the Central African Republic, the Congo Republic, and, since 1985, Equatorial Guinea—the former members of the federation of the AEF supplemented by Cameroon and Equatorial Guinea. The UDEAC was designed to provide its members with the advantages of economic union. Through UDEAC, Gabon gains direct access to surrounding markets and sources of foodstuffs and other commodities that are not subject to severe taxation. The UDEAC is, additionally, an important instrument of economic coordination in central Africa. Through its historic relationship with France, UDEAC is an associate member of the EEC, a relationship that facilitates economic interactions with the countries of western Europe and, predictably, gives special advantages to the French in central Africa. UDEAC's Development Bank of Central African States, located in Brazzaville, is an intermediary for the distribution of EEC funds for development projects in the member states. Although the federation passed through several periods of difficulty, it remains intact: In 1968, Chad and the Central African Republic withdrew from UDEAC under pressure from Zaire to create a new economic union; both countries have been readmitted, and the headquarters of the organization is now located in Bangui, the capital of the Central African Republic. Membership in the Communauté économique des états de l'Afrique centrale (CEEAC) provides the Gabonese with a broader base of inter-African economic involvement. In addition to the member states of the UDEAC, the CEEAC includes Zaire, Rwanda, Burundi, and São Tomé and Príncipe.

Bongo ended Gabon's relationship with the Organization commune africaine et malgache (OCAM), an early venture in francophone cooperation initiated by President Léon Mba in 1961. For Gabon, the most significant component of the OCAM agreement was the joint operation of Air Afrique. Gabon participated in OCAM until 1976, when it decided to create its own national airline, Air Gabon. Gabon's decision to leave OCAM was reportedly due to the organization's decision not to offer a major administrative position to a Gabonese national.

GABON AND WESTERN EUROPE

Gabon receives substantial assistance from Europe. Since 1970, the EEC, through the European Development Bank, provided Gabon with nearly U.S.$30 million, primarily for the development and construction of the Transgabonais. In the case of the EEC, Gabon benefits directly from its historical association with France and UDEAC's associate membership status in the EEC. With the completion of the major Transgabonais construction phases, EEC funds have been granted to improve other components of Gabon's transportation infrastructure and the public water systems in Libreville and Port Gentil, and to construct the new mineral port at Owendo.[6]

After France, West Germany provides Gabon with the most extensive and diversified forms of assistance. West German capital was instrumental in the construction of the Transgabonais and the West German government provides 10 percent of the capital of the Gabonese Development Bank. German firms constructed bridges at Tchibanga and Mouila, German technicians installed radio facilities in the city of Oyem in the Woleu N'Tem, and the German government provided DM 10 million (U.S.$6.1 million) for the construction of the Hotel Dialogue in Libreville. A number of private firms, notably Hobum-Afrika, are involved with the Gabonese government and other private investors in other development projects.[7]

Italy and Great Britain are two other European countries involved in providing capital and technical assistance to Gabon. Italy purchases Gabonese uranium, and, through EUROTRAG, provided credits for purchases of equipment for the Transgabonais. Although not extensive, the British presence is notable for its longevity. The British firms John Holt and Hatton and Cookson have been in Gabon since the 1800s and remain involved in the distribution of a variety of products, notably textiles and automobiles. The British government accorded credits of £25 million (U.S.$45 million) for matériel for the Transgabonais, and the British firms Woodrow and Wimpey International, took part in financing the railway's second phase. The British also have concluded agreements with the Gabonese for the development of mining technology.

GABON, THE USSR, AND EASTERN EUROPE

Until 1985, Gabon's relations with the Soviet Union were minimal. Although the Soviet Union has maintained an embassy in Gabon since 1970, its presence was essentially symbolic and limited to cultural programs and small commercial exchanges. In 1986, however, the Soviet government began purchasing Gabonese manganese and entered into an agreement to provide low-interest loans for the construction of manganese, steel, and iron facilities. Gabon's decision to diversify and strengthen the nonpetroleum sector of the economy could lead to more involvement with the Soviet Union, if current political and economic difficulties in the Soviet Union permit. Bongo's earlier fears of communist subversion appear to have disappeared.

Gabon has courted the assistance of other eastern European countries since the mid-1970s and concluded technical assistance pacts with Romania, Czechoslovakia, Yugoslavia, and to a significantly lesser degree, East Germany. In 1979, the governments of Romania and Gabon signed a friendship treaty establishing the Romania-Gabon Commission with offices in Libreville and Bucharest. Romania provided funds to Gabon for the purchase of railway cars for the Transgabonais and contributed to the construction of a factory for the production of railway ties. The Yugoslav presence in Gabon is highly visible. A Yugoslav firm, Autoput, paved the major streets of Libreville and Port Gentil; the conference center for the 1977 OAU conference and the Libreville city hall were projects of another Yugoslav firm, Energoprojekt. East German participation has been limited to financial contributions to the Albert Schweitzer hospital in Lambaréné.

In its relations with the countries of eastern Europe and with the Soviet Union, the Bongo government has been pragmatic, entering into agreements to implement its primary goal of building the Transgabonais and obtain the support services required to complete that work. In the process, Gabon appears not to have sacrificed its flexibility or autonomy. In fact, it seems that Gabon's ventures beyond the traditional parameters of francophone relations have paid significant dividends.[8]

GABON AND ISLAM

One of the most interesting events in recent Gabonese history was President Bongo's conversion to Islam in 1973 (he adopted the name El Hadj Omar Bongo after the prescribed trip to Mecca). Bongo's conversion was regarded by many observers as diplomatic, and he has actively pursued a role within the community of Arab states. Gabon is not a part of Muslim Africa—the small Islamic community in Gabon is composed primarily of expatriate Senegalese, Malians, and others—but it was widely assumed that conversion would give Bongo access to the wealth of the Arab states to carry out his vow to build the Transgabonais at any price. Although Gabon has not been overwhelmed by funds from the Arab community, Bongo has forged several connections that appear to have enhanced his role and stature in the affairs of the continent.

Bongo's friendliness with the Libyan regime of Moammar Qaddafi conjured up the vision of vast economic benefits for Gabon. During Bongo's highly publicized trip to Libya in 1973, he and Qaddafi concluded an assistance agreement. It was abrogated abruptly only a year later, however, and the only real legacy of Bongo's short-lived relationship with Libya may be the apparently successful role of intermediary that Bongo energetically assumed in Libya's dispute with Chad. Although circumstances changed again dramatically in Chad in early 1991, Bongo's rapport with the Libyans could facilitate a general rapprochement between the Libyans and several countries of the Sahel region fearful of possible Libyan aggression.

Gabon's relationship with Morocco may be one of the most significant results of Bongo's lobbying within the Muslim community. Hassan of Morocco and Bongo have established a close personal relationship, and Moroccan technical assistance to Gabon dramatically increased over the 1980s. Moroccan officers are involved in the training and command of Bongo's presidential guard, and a Moroccan training mission provides assistance to the Gabonese military forces. The Moroccan government provides financial and technical assistance for telecommunications, tourism, and real estate development through the Gabonese bank, Crédit immobilier du Gabon. Hassan also provided the funds for the construction of a mosque in Libreville. Bongo considers Morocco a close ally and has supported Morocco's claims in the conflict with Algeria over disputed lands in the western Sahara.

Gabon also enjoys excellent relations with Algeria (despite Bongo's support of Morocco in the western Sahara conflict) and with Tunisia. Among the first of the African countries to support Gabon's decision to build the Transgabonais, Algeria provided construction funds and assisted in the installation of signal equipment. Gabon and Tunisia have concluded several economic and technical agreements in public health, industry, and electronics.

Bongo's most significant venture may be his involvement with the OPEC nations, a relationship that was, in all likelihood, enhanced by his conversion to Islam. Although Gabon is not one of the major OPEC producers, the withdrawal of Iran as a major supplier and the Persian Gulf crisis of 1990 both enhanced Gabon's position in the hierarchy of oil-producing countries. Membership in OPEC provides the Gabonese with a voice in the critical pricing decisions that have determined the world price for petroleum since the early 1970s. Gabon became an associate member of OPEC in 1974, following OPEC's embargo against Israel's supporters, and a full member of the organization in 1975. Gabon derives both political and economic stability from its OPEC membership. OPEC's 1988 decision in Vienna to raise production levels and prices provided an important corrective for the gradual decline in Gabonese production and revenue. Similarly, Iraq's invasion of Kuwait in the late summer of 1990 brought about an increase in Gabonese production that has helped to alleviate the recent budget problems.

Gabon's membership in OPEC has also led to direct financial assistance from the OPEC countries. Between 1980 and 1986, Gabon received U.S.$1.1 million from the Arab member states, and U.S.$21 million from the combined OPEC membership. This Arab assistance in financing the Transgabonais necessarily led to a shift in Gabon's relationship with Israel. Before the Arab-Israeli war of 1973 and Gabon's concerted search for funds in the Arab world in the early 1970s, Gabon and Israel were involved in several technical assistance agreements, most notably in forestry and agricultural development. Gabon broke diplomatic relations with Israel in 1973, aligning itself with the Arab bloc of OPEC countries that initiated the embargo of petroleum sales to the United States and western Europe. (One report had it that Gabon's break with Israel was prompted by Josephine Bongo's anger at being snubbed by Israeli Prime Minister Golda Meir during a trip to Jerusalem.)[9]

GABON, CHINA, AND THE PACIFIC RIM

Gabon established diplomatic relations with China in 1974. Since then, Bongo has visited China five times, and the two countries have concluded a number of bilateral assistance agreements. In light of Bongo's conservatism, a Gabonese relationship with China could be considered as a contradiction. Bongo appears to admire the Chinese for their nonaligned stance and to view China and Gabon as developing nations with similar positions on major issues. China has provided such assistance to Gabon as an experimental rice station near Kango, in the estuary region, and the development of medical clinics in rural areas. China buys Gabonese manganese as part of a trade relationship that exceeded U.S.$20 million in 1986 and is expected to increase. Although the Chinese presence is modest, it is significant that trade with China has increased steadily since 1974 and that Gabon was included in Premier Zhao Ziyand's twenty-nation tour of Africa in 1983. For Gabon, China is a future market of enormous proportions for Gabon's strategic exports. Bongo also appears to be attracted by the tremendous energy and accomplishments of the Chinese in developing a self-sufficient economy. It is certainly Gabon's goal to emulate the Chinese, and their moral and economic support are welcomed in Gabon.

Gabon has also expanded its ties with the other major industrial powers of the Pacific Rim—Japan and the Republic of South Korea. There is a small Korean community in Libreville, and Bongo has sought Japanese investment in a number of diversification projects. The Koreans financed and constructed a fifteen-story department store and office building, Rénovation, in downtown Libreville, and the distribution network for both Korean and Japanese automobiles and trucks expanded rapidly in the 1980s. The Gabonese have concluded an agreement with the Koreans for railway cars for the Transgabonais and the Korean Electric Company is exploring for new manganese deposits.

Japan's involvement with Gabon is increasing. The Japanese extended credits for the purchase of equipment for the Transgabonais and are involved in expanding the production of rice. The Nuclear Power Company of Japan has undertaken uranium exploration in the estuary region and several other sites in the country. The Japanese and Korean presence, although modest, illustrates Bongo's attempt to seek new markets for Gabonese products and broaden the investment base of the Gabonese economy.[10]

GABON AND THE UNITED STATES

For many years, the French sought to exclude the United States from Gabonese affairs. In fact, Gabon's relationship with the United States became problematic following the coup of 1964 when Mba's French advisers attempted to convince him that the U.S. Central Intelligence Agency (CIA) was involved in the attempt to overthrow the regime. In 1972, Bongo reversed his 1968 decision to expel U.S. Peace Corps volunteers, a shift that coincided with Bongo's vow to build the Transgabonais at any cost, and concerted efforts to secure U.S. financial assistance. The Gabonese succeeded in securing U.S. assistance, and Bongo brought in U.S. engineering firms for initial feasibility studies. Despite the refusal of Robert McNamara, president of the World Bank, to support the venture, the U.S. Export/Import Bank, Citicorp, and Chase Manhattan provided funds for a number of construction projects as well as matériel for the railroad. With the rapid increase in petroleum income between 1973 and 1975, Bongo concluded defiantly that the Gabonese could undertake the construction of the Transgabonais without the participation of the World Bank or the IMF.

Since 1972, U.S. firms have established an important presence in Gabon, and in the 1980s the United States became an important market for Gabon's exports. Paralleling the French, U.S. interests in Gabon are focused primarily on mining and petroleum exploration. Bethlehem Steel and U.S. Steel were early entrants. Bethlehem Steel is a major partner in the Société des mines de fer de Mékambo (SOMIFER), the iron consortium, and U.S. Steel presently holds 36.4 percent of the stock of COMILOG, the firm that mines and distributes Gabonese manganese. Petroleum production is the current area of interest for U.S. firms. In the post–World War II period, the production and development of Gabonese petroleum was monopolized by the French through their Gabonese intermediary, Elf Gabon. In the early 1960s, when preliminary soundings indicated the existence of vast offshore reserves, the number of interested firms, U.S. and European, increased rapidly. AMOCO, Océan, Murphy, Gulf, Mobil, and Tenneco are now engaged in exploration and production. Although Tenneco's Gabonese assets have been purchased by British Petroleum, the U.S. presence remains substantial.

U.S. influence in Gabon has clearly grown since 1970. U.S. advisers are now closely involved in Gabon's economic plans, and consultations with U.S. officials and private firms are routine. In fact, the Bongo government undertook a concerted public relations campaign to convince U.S. companies to invest in Gabon. Pierre Péan notes in *Affaires africaines* that the U.S. industrialist, Armand Hammer of Occidental Petroleum, who died in fall 1990, was a prominent member of Bongo's inner circle.[11]

Bongo has visited the United States several times, most recently in 1988; he often reminds those who question him about his relationship with the United States that he was the first African head of state to meet with President Jimmy Carter in 1976. During Bongo's visit to Washington in 1988, he and President Ronald Reagan discussed a variety of African issues, including Bongo's role in mediating the dispute between Libya and Chad over territory in the northern Sahara. While in Washington, Bongo concluded an agreement for a longer period of payment on Gabon's U.S.$7 million purchases of U.S. military equipment. A second agreement, for U.S. training for Gabonese pilots, represented a dramatic reversal of traditional French dominance in Gabonese military aviation.

The increasing presence of the United States in Gabon marks a significant shift in the attitude of U.S. policy planners toward Gabon. Following the 1964 coup and French accusations of CIA involvement, Gabon was forgotten until Bongo's decision to build the Transgabonais. The return of the Peace Corps to Gabon and subsequent U.S. involvement in mining and petroleum production represent the restoration of a significant U.S. presence in the country. Gabon's small size limits its attractiveness as a consumer of U.S. goods, however, and the strategic interests of the United States do not require a large, visible presence.[12] It seems unlikely that the United States will overwhelm more than a century of the *mission civilatrice*. Although Bongo will exploit any possibility to keep the French off balance, it is difficult to believe that Gabon would willingly substitute U.S. hegemony for the more familiar French version.

GABON AND CANADA

Since 1986, relations between Gabon and Canada appear to have entered a new period of cooperation. In 1985, in an incident reminiscent of de Gaulle's expression of support for a free Quebec, Gabon invited the Quebecois Minister of Culture to participate in a summit conference of francophone countries in Libreville. The move angered the Canadian government and relations between the two governments reached a virtual standstill. But after a cooling-off period, Canada and Gabon concluded a number of cooperation agreements, and Canada now purchases a significant volume of Gabonese manganese and petroleum. Although several projects were postponed because of Gabon's austerity program, plans were drawn up for Canadians to construct the proposed new Ministry of

Foreign Affairs building in Libreville, and two Canadian firms—Watts, Grits & McOuat and Boundar Clegg & Company—are under contract with the Gabonese government to perform an extensive mineral survey along the route of the Transgabonais.[13] In the rural areas of northern Gabon, Canadian *coopérants* are involved in a project called Media Villages—a program to install solar energy facilities and instructional television for Gabonese farmers. Many of the Canadian technicians and teachers are from Quebec, and the francophone connection creates an obvious advantage for the Canadians in their relationship with the Gabonese.

GABON AND LATIN AMERICA

As part of its effort to reduce dependency on France and diversify its sources of goods and services, Gabon has aggressively pursued economic relations with a number of Latin American nations, most notably, Brazil. Gabon purchases military matériel destined for Bongo's presidential guard from Brazilian firms, and the two governments are parties to an agreement to market a variety of Brazilian products in Gabon. Although Gabon's current climate of austerity precludes any significant new ventures, plans are in the works for cooperative agreements with Mexico and Argentina.

CONCLUSION

Overall, Gabon's foreign policy in the 1980s represents a concerted effort to retain the benefits of the historic relationship with France and a growing impatience about the constraints imposed by the relationship. The Gabonese are aware that French colonial exploitation of their natural resources distorted their economy; the imbalance between agricultural production and imports, for example, results directly from the French involvement, and Gabon's efforts to redefine its relationship with France are undermined by the very nature of the relationship. Under Bongo's leadership, members of the Gabonese elite and others drawn to the country because of its wealth have enriched themselves at the expense of the country. It is equally apparent that the French are implicated in this tale of exploitation. Their preoccupation with their apparent strategic needs and a decided predisposition to look the other way have placed a substantial burden on the people of Gabon. Although Gabon's relations with the external world are often marred by xenophobia and opportunism, one can only sympathize with the country's goals of autonomy and self-sufficiency. It may be that the next generation of Gabonese, nurtured in a spirit of pluralism and democracy, will have the determination to create a better future.

NOTES

1. For an account of the confrontation, see Siradiou Diallo, "Une crise de plus?" *Jeune Afrique,* no. 1196 (December 7, 1983), pp. 38–43.

2. "Gabon: Money for Taking," *Africa Confidential,* 25, no. 16 (April 1984), p. 7.

3. *Le Monde hebdomadaire* (Paris), June 14–20, 1990.

4. Pierre Péan, *Affaires africaines* (Paris: Fayard, 1983), pp. 71–92.

5. Material in this section compiled from EIU Country Reports, *Congo, Gabon, Equatorial Guinea,* 1986–1990; *Africa Confidential,* 1986–1990 and *Marchés tropicaux et méditérranéens,* 1986–1990.

6. OECD, *Geographical Distribution of Financial Flows to Developing Countries* (Paris: OECD Publications Service, 1991), pp. 122–123.

7. EIU Country Profile, *Gabon, 1986–87,* pp. 8–10.

8. EIU Country Profiles, *Gabon,* 1986–1990.

9. "Gabon 1981," *Marchés tropicaux et méditérranéens* (special edition) 31, no. 1881 (November 27, 1981), pp. 3129–3131.

10. EIU Country Profiles, *Gabon,* 1986–1990.

11. Péan, *Affaires africaines,* p. 98.

12. Charles B. Darlington and Alice F. Darlington, *African Betrayal* (New York: David McKay, 1968), pp. 101–125.

13. EIU Country Report, *Congo, Gabon, Equatorial Guinea,* no. 1 (1990), p. 30.

6
Looking to the Future

With their initial steps in the direction of multipartyism and political democracy, the Gabonese have passed an important milestone. Although the return to an authoritarian system should not be ruled out, the process of change has begun, and unless the participants themselves lose sight of their goals, the future of Gabonese democracy appears promising. It is certain, nevertheless, that Gabon's course will not be an uneventful one.

THE POLITICAL ENVIRONMENT

It is immediately apparent that Gabon's authoritarian political culture may not be conducive to the development of democracy and pluralism without turmoil. On one hand, the motives of the incumbent president are not clear, and on the other, the structure of interests associated with the système Bongo can be expected to resist any substantial shifts in the direction of policy that could be harmful to the interests of the *clan des gabonais*. While President Bongo can be expected to carry out his pledge to remain above the parties and the legislature, it is totally naive to expect that those who have prospered during the Bongo era will submit passively to any change in the pattern of rewards established since 1960. It is also worth noting that issues of pluralism and democracy extend beyond the formalities of voting and elections. The Bongo regime, for example, is not accustomed to criticism or rough-and-tumble parliamentary politics. Will an opposition press endure? This is an ideal moment for Makaya to be joined by many Gabonese voices, but that possibility must await the resolution of several basic issues of power.

Throughout the period of independence, Gabon's leadership has been preoccupied with maintaining an orderly, stable political environment. The price of order and stability has been high: Arrests and deportations resulting from rather mild criticisms of the regime and its primary figures have been frequent occurrences among the Gabonese and the expatriate community. The regime's congenial public face conceals a

139

system of power and privilege that has maintained itself through intimidation and, possibly, murder and assassination. Bongo supporters in France were implicated in the bombing of Pierre Péan's Paris residence following the publication of *Affaires africaines,* CEDOC is well known to the international human rights community, and repeated charges of corruption and fraudulent practices continue to erode public confidence in the government. From this perspective, the Gabonese have a compelling obligation to dismantle an authoritarian machine that has stifled the development of the habits and practices of democratic politics. There is a corresponding danger that an overly narrow focus on open elections will convince those who are misled by the trappings of democracy that the regime is moving in the right direction. The motives of the regime may, in fact, be benign, but a few hastily called elections do not constitute a victory for democracy; they should be viewed as one part of a more substantial process that will require fundamental changes in the assumptions about Gabonese politics, the role and responsibilities of government, and, perhaps, the resolution of the long-standing debate about the incompatibility of African traditions and political democracy. There is, indeed, cause for optimism, but also ample room for pessimistic conclusions.

Since his inauguration in 1967 as the second president of the republic, Bongo has held the fortunes of the Gabonese people in his hands; it has been apparent all the while that Bongo commands the Gabonese ship of state. The burden of the moment falls upon him to fulfill his pledge to bring democracy to Gabon, but it falls as well on those who have a corresponding obligation to conduct their affairs in the same spirit. Among the dangers confronting Gabon's democratic future, ethnic tensions and divisiveness represent an important challenge. Although it is, perhaps, inevitable that ethnicity divide the Gabonese from each other, only a system that acknowledges the persistence of ethnicity will be likely to surmount its obstacles. Before Joseph Rendjame's death in May 1990 and the ensuing disturbances in Libreville and Port Gentil, there was considerable speculation about the possibility of Bongo acknowledging the central role of Gabon's leading ethnic groups and distributing the major positions of the government and legislature according to an ethnic formula. Bongo can also be expected to undertake efforts to retain the PDG as the major instrument of his political power. Would such an approach be only another example of Bongo's practiced skill at ethnic balance and a premeditated attempt to retain power by sharing its spoils? Or could the recognition of a more positive sense of ethnicity form the basis for a constitutional sharing of power that could remedy the worst abuses of the system of ethnic patronage? It is apparent that any discussion of the future disposition of power in Gabon must recognize the aspirations of the Fang, possibly at the expense of smaller groups like Bongo's Téké kin, who have received socioeconomic and political benefits disproportionate to their numbers. It seems likely that the prime ministership will be held by a Fang, with other groups sharing in the distribution of Gabon's tradition-ally large ministerial contingent.

Given its complex ethnic configuration and the political and geo-graphical divisions based on ethnicity, Gabon virtually cries out for a consociational solution, that is, a political arrangement that formally acknowledges the legitimacy of ethnic and linguistic diversity and incor-porates them into the constitutional structure.[1] In consociational govern-ment and politics, ethnicity holds its ground, and groups that share in the constitutional distribution of power consciously forfeit their "right" to aggregate power in rigid majoritarian-minoritarian terms and rule in the name of the numerically powerful. Certainly, the situation in Gabon, specifically in the short term, requires an acknowledgment of Fang claims and those of previously disenfranchised groups like the Bapounou and Eshira, whose periodic displays of discontent illustrate frustration with their dual identities as Bapounou or Eshira *and* Gabonese. Although this persistent duality is an obvious problem, it could also, paradoxically, be a significant dimension of a solution. On this point, the Gabonese are not alone in their efforts to sustain a polity in an institutional framework that is not conducive to ethnic harmony. In 1991, Yugoslavia appears on the brink of disintegration, and the cacophany of ethnic voices from the Soviet Union has virtually drowned out calls for national unity and cooperation; Aleksandr Solzhenitsyn's embittered demand for a Slavic republic under-scores the dramatic and sudden resurrection of muted voices and concerns in the post–cold war era. Within the vastness of the Soviet Union and in the ethnically divided Yugoslav republic, calls for autonomy represent long-standing nationalist claims earlier submerged in the pursuit of other aims. In a different context, Quebec's demands on the Canadian federation illustrate another reach of contemporary nationalist sentiments. The recent past provides scores of examples of the tensions and rivalries within and between nation-states based on religion or language: The existence of Pakistan and Bangladesh speak to the deep chasms created by religion, and within the boundaries of such an outwardly stable democracy as Belgium, Flemish-Walloon rivalries divide the city of Brussels into hostile camps. It would certainly appear that the future of many places in the world depends upon their ability to extract strength and unity from diversity.

Gabon's heterogeneity may very well be the source of its future vitality. It is, nevertheless, the specific responsibility of the Gabonese governing class to move beyond a narrowly defined ethnic politics, in which the fruits of participation and cooperation extend only to those who are coopted into the exclusive ranks of the elite. If pluralism and multiparty democracy are viewed only as techniques to acquire wealth and privilege, rather than the means to institute an important discourse about the public interest, the Gabonese may never escape the tensions and uncertainties of the past. Reports that opposition leaders appropriated for their personal use electoral funds provided by the government during the 1990 elections only reinforces the view of those who remain fundamentally skeptical about any change in the business-as-usual attitude of the Gabonese governing class.

ECONOMIC PROSPECTS

It is axiomatic that Gabon's political future is dependent on its economy and the quality of its relationships with France and, secondarily, the United States. From this perspective, there are indications of a promising future accompanied by a few critical warning signs.

Events outside Gabon have given an unexpected boost to Gabon's petroleum-based economy. Increased purchases of petroleum throughout the 1980s by Canada and the United States provided a valuable buffer during the period of austerity. Similarly, the Persian Gulf crisis of 1990–1991, and the resulting demand for petroleum to compensate for the diminished supply from Kuwait and Iraq occurred at an opportune moment for Gabon, enabling the Gabonese to double their production to 350,000 barrels per day. This level of production allowed the regime to eliminate the most unpopular features of its austerity program; the 3 percent "solidarity tax" on civil service salaries has been dropped and the general freeze on wages and salaries partially rescinded.

Gabon's dependency on petroleum may, however, at any moment, lead to a repeat of the near-disastrous circumstances of 1986. The petroleum sector of the economy appears to have been restored to its previous level of revenue production, and the unanticipated gains, buttressed by Gabon's favorable relationship with its creditors and the IMF, provide critical stability for Gabon's immediate economic future. Gabon is clearly not the poorest of the poor, and its relative economic well-being removes it from the list of the world's neediest aid recipients. But the Gabonese economy relies on products that are extremely vulnerable to substantial shifts in demand, and recent events have created a number of potentially serious circumstances. Gabon's external debt currently surpasses F CFA 800 billion (nearly U.S.$3 billion), and despite revised payment schedules, the burden of repayment will weigh heavily for many years. The volatility of markets has, in addition—and without much public notice—produced a large pool of unemployed workers. In November 1990, nearly 12 percent of the work force was unemployed, with increasing unemployment expected as timber and manganese sales decline.[2] It is apparent, as well, that any worsening of the economic situation will exacerbate ethnic and regional tensions and the currently tense relations between the Gabonese and the large contingent of expatriate workers.

The most serious challenge to Gabon's economic and political stability may arrive from an entirely unanticipated direction, however. France's preparations for the next stage of EEC expansion in 1992 and the rapid changes in the economic and political environment of the Soviet Union and eastern Europe have fostered a French review of its African policies. Since the early twentieth century, France's contacts with Africa have remained essentially within francophone parameters. Population and economic giants like Nigeria have been outside the reach of French interests (de Gaulle's support of Biafran secession further distanced France from Nigeria). France now appears intent upon enlarging its circle of African economic partners, possibly leading to a reformulation of its relations with its former colonies. In this vein, the French government has engaged in discussions focusing on the future of the franc zone, and French discussions with Zaire, clearly facilitated by the francophone connection, as well as increasing assistance to Ghana suggest that the French are no longer content to deal exclusively with their former colonies. In view of these initiatives, Gabon's interests would be well served by decisive efforts to complete its diversification projects, and, as Pierre Claver Maganga-Moussavou urged, to aggressively attack its problems of agricultural production. From the perspective of economic resources, Gabon, of all the former French colonies in Africa, has the greatest potential for an economic future in which the French might wish to limit their investments and obligations. Gabonese options include the possibility of more extensive economic contacts with the United States, Canada, and Latin America, and Gabon's strategic resources are potentially attractive in a number of international markets.

It is highly doubtful that the French would abandon or seriously damage their relationship with the Gabonese. On several occasions, the French have appeared apprehensive about efforts by the United States to expand contacts with Gabon. The French embassy in Washington monitors Congressional contacts with the Gabonese National Assembly, and a decision by President Bongo to engage the Bechtel Corporation for assistance in the development of the regime's economic policies was reported to have disturbed the Mitterrand government.[3] This pattern of events suggests that Gabon will continue to attract the attention of both France and the United States. The critical question for the 1990s is whether or not the Gabonese themselves will be in a position to fully enjoy the potential fruits of Franco-American competition. If they are not to continue as a neocolonial enclave, the Gabonese must come to terms with their dependency and critically assess their options. The future of the Gabonese state is also partly in the hands of France, the United States, and the international monetary community. Gabon's authoritarian system survived because the outward signs of stability and order pleased those who rate their investments higher than political and economic justice, and if the Gabonese fail in their efforts to implement a multiparty democracy, the fault will not be solely theirs.

NOTES

1. For an overview of the discussion and literature on consociational government and politics, see Arend Lijphart, *Democracy in Plural Societies: A Comparative Exploration* (New Haven, Conn.: Yale University Press, 1977); and Kenneth McRae, ed., *Consociational Democracy: Political Accommodation in Segmented Societies* (Ottawa: Carleton Library, 1974). For an analysis of a specific consociational arrangement, see Jürg Steiner, *Amicable Agreement versus Majority Rule: Conflict Resolution in Switzerland* (Chapel Hill: University of North Carolina Press, 1974).

2. Francis Kpatindé, "Le Gabon entre Bongo et les Bûcherons," *Jeune Afrique*, no. 1558 (December 7–13, 1990), p. 29.

3. "Gabon: Rivalité franco-americaine," *Jeune Afrique*, no. 1553 (October 3–9, 1990), p. 4.

Selected Bibliography

Aicardi, Marc de Saint-Paul. *Gabon: The Development of a Nation.* London: Routledge, 1989. Published in French as *Le Gabon: du roi Denis à Omar Bongo.* Paris: Albatros, 1987.

Ambouroue-Avaro, Joseph. *Un peuple gabonais à l'aube de la colonisation.* Paris: Editions Karthala, 1981.

Amnesty International. *Gabon: Déni de justice au cours d'un procès.* London: Amnesty International Publications, 1984.

Assam, Aristote. *Omar Bongo, ou la racine du mal gabonais.* Paris: Pensée universelle, 1985.

Bakajika, Banjakila. "Les ancêtres des Bantu vivaient-ils au Tchad ou au Shaba?" *Afrique histoire,* no.9 (1983): 17–22.

Balandier, Georges. *Sociologie actuelle de l'Afrique noire: Dynamique sociale en Afrique centrale.* Paris: Quadrige/Presses universitaire de France, 1982.

Biffot, Laurent. "Genèse des classes sociales au Gabon." *Annales de l'Ecole Nationale d'Administration* (Libreville) 2 (1977): 33–48.

Bouquerel, Jacqueline. *Le Gabon.* Paris: Que sais-je?/Presses universitaire de France, 1976.

Brooke, James. "African Railroad Running a Deficit." *New York Times,* May 23, 1988.

Brunschwig, Henri. *French Exploration in Tropical Africa from 1865–1898.* In P. Duignan, and L. H. Gann, *The History and Politics of Colonialism, 1870–1914,* pp. 132–164. London: Cambridge University Press, 1969.

Bucher, Henry. "The Mpongwé of the Gabon Estuary." Ph.D. diss., University of Wisconsin–Madison, 1977.

Cabrol, Claude. "Notes sur les pygmées de Mékambo." Gabon National Library. Mimeo, 1962.

Compte, Gilbert. "La république gabonaise: Treize années d'histoire." *Revue française d'études politiques africaines* 90 (June 1973): 39–57.

Coquery-Vidrovitch, Catherine. *Le Congo au temps des grandes compagnies concessionaires, 1898–1930.* Paris: Mouton, 1972.

———. *French Colonization in Africa to 1920: Administration and Development.* In P. Duignan and L. H. Gann, *The History and Politics of Colonialism, 1870–1914,* pp. 165–198. London: Cambridge University Press, 1969.

145

Darlington, Charles B.; and Darlington, Alice F. *African Betrayal*. New York: David McKay, 1968.

Deschamps, Hubert. "Quinze ans de Gabon: Les débuts de l'établissement français, 1839–1853." *Revue d'histoire d'outre-mer* 50, no. 180–181 (1965).

Diallo, Siradiou."Une crise de plus?" *Jeune Afrique*, no. 1196 (December 7, 1983): 38–43.

Digombe, Lazare; Locko, Michel; and Emejulu, James. "Nouvelles recherches archeologiques à Ikengué (Fernan Vaz, Province de l'Ogouée-Maritime, Gabon): Un site datant de 1300 B.C." *L'Anthropologie* (Paris) 91, no. 2 (1987): 705–710.

Diop, Cheikh Anta. *Pre-Colonial Black Africa*. Westport, Conn.: Lawrence Hill, 1987.

Duhamel, Olivier. "Le parti démocratique gabonais." *Revue française d'études politiques africaines*, no. 125 (May 1976): 24–27.

Duignan, P.; and Gann, L. H. *The History and Politics of Colonialism, 1870–1914*. London: Cambridge University Press, 1969.

Eboué, Félix. *La nouvelle politique indigène*. Brazzaville: Afrique française libre, 1941.

Essone-Ndong, Laurent. "Les syndicats du Gabon." *Annales de l'école nationale d'administration* (Libreville) 1 (1977): 47–53.

Fernandez, James. *Bwiti: An Ethnography of the Religious Imagination in Africa*. Princeton, N.J.: Princeton University Press, 1982.

Gardinier, David E. *Historical Dictionary of Gabon*. Metuchen, N.J.: Scarecrow Press, 1981.

Gaulme, François. *Le Gabon et son ombre*. Paris: Editions Karthala, 1988.

———. *Le Pays du Cama: Un ancien état Côtier du Gabon et ses origines*. Paris: Editions Karthala, 1981.

Greisheimer, Lawrence. "Ministers get their TV come-uppance in Gabon." *Manchester Guardian Weekly* (January 5, 1986): 12.

Guez, Nicole. "Gabon-France: La méprise." *Jeune Afrique économie* (bi-mensuel), no. 28 (December 8, 1983): 15–18.

Hargreaves, John P. *Prelude to the Partition of West Africa*. New York: St. Martin's Press, 1970.

Hervouet, François. "Le processus de concentration des pouvoirs par le président de la république au Gabon." *Penant: Revue de droit des pays d'Afrique*, no. 779 (January–March 1983): 1–35.

International Labour Organization. *L'emploi et répartition des revenus dans la république gabonaise*. Addis Ababa: International Labour Office, 1984.

Kim, Sung Ho. "Intervention at the Request of Incumbent Governments." Ph.D. diss., Columbia University, 1974.

Kpatindé, Francis."Portrait: Paul Mba Abbesole—les parcours sinuex d'un opposant dans l'âme." *Jeune Afrique*, no. 1563 (December 12–18, 1990): 28–29.

———. "Le Gabon entre Bongo et les Bûcherons." *Jeune Afrique*, no. 1558 (November 7–13, 1990): 28–29.

Lijphart, Arend. *Democracy in Plural Societies: A Comparative Exploration*. New Haven, Conn.: Yale University Press, 1977.

Maganga-Moussavou, Pierre Claver. *Economic Development: Does Aid Help? A Case Study of French Development Assistance to Gabon.* Edited by Barbara J. Sims. Washington, D.C.: African Communications Liaison Service, 1983.

——. *L'aide publique de la France au développement du Gabon depuis l'indépendance.* Paris: Publications de la Sorbonne, 1982.

Manning, Patrick. *Francophone Sub-Saharan Africa, 1880–1985.* New York: Cambridge University Press, 1988.

Marshall, D. Bruce. *The French Colonial Myth and Constitution-Making in the Fourth Republic.* New Haven, Conn.: Yale University Press, 1973.

M'Bokolo, Elikia. *Noirs et blancs en Afrique equatoriale: Les sociétés côtières et la pénétration française vers 1820–1874.* Paris: Mouton, 1981.

——. *Le roi Denis: La première tentative de modernisation de Gabon.* Dakar: Nouvelles éditions africaines, 1976.

McRae, Kenneth, ed. *Consociational Democracy: Political Accommodation in Segmented Societies.* Ottawa: Carleton Library, 1974.

Metegue-N'Nah, Nicolas. *L'implantation coloniale au Gabon: Résistance d'un peuple.* Vol. 1. Paris: Harmattan, 1981.

——. *Economies et sociétés au Gabon dans la premières moitié du XXeme siècle.* Paris: Harmattan, 1979.

Meyo-Bibang, Frédéric. *Le Gabon.* Paris: Hatier, 1975.

——. *Aperçu historique du Gabon.* Libreville: Institut pedagogique national, 1973.

Ministère de l'éducation nationale de la république gabonaise. *Géographie et cartographie du Gabon.* Paris: Editions classique d'expression française, 1981.

Nkoghve-Mve, Moïse. "Le Docteur Schweitzer et la colonisation." *Réalités gabonaises* (January–February, 1977): 21–26.

Pabanel, Jean-Pierre. *Les coups d'état militaires en Afrique noire.* Paris: Harmattan, 1984.

Pallard, Joachim. "Evénements des 18, 19, et 20 Février, 1964." Gabon National Archives. Memorandum, February 20, 1964.

Patterson, Karl David. *The Northern Gabon Coast to 1875.* Oxford: Clarendon Press, 1975.

Péan, Pierre. *Affaires africaines.* Paris: Fayard, 1983.

Poissonier, Ariane. "Faites l'amour et pas la mort." *Jeune Afrique*, no. 1561 (November 28–December 4, 1990): 36–37.

Raponda-Walker, André. *Notes d'histoire du Gabon.* Montpellier: Institut d'études centrafricaines, 1960.

Raponda-Walker, André, and Sillans, Roger. *Rites et croyances des peuples du Gabon.* Paris: Présence africaine, 1962.

Ratanga-Atoz, Ange. *Initiation à l'histoire générale du Gabon.* Libreville: Ministère de l'éducation nationale/Université Omar Bongo, 1979.

——. "Commerce, economie et société dans le Gabon du XIXeme–début XXeme siècle." *Annales de l'école nationale d'administration* (Libreville) 2 (1977): 85–96.

Reed, Michael C. "Gabon: A Neo-Colonial Enclave of Enduring French Interests." *Journal of Modern African Studies* 25, no. 2 (1987): 283–320.

Segal, Ronald. *African Profiles*. New York: Penguin Books, 1962.

Schnapper, Bernard. *La politique et le commerce français dans la golfe du Guinée de 1838 à 1871*. Paris: Mouton, 1961.

Schweitzer, Albert. *From My African Notebook*. London: Allen and Unwin, 1938.

———. *More From the Primeval Forest*. London: Allen and Unwin, 1931.

Spero, Joan. "Dominance-Dependence Relationship: The Case of France and Gabon." Ph.D. diss., Columbia University, 1973.

Thompson, Virginia; and Adloff, Richard. *The Emerging States of Equatorial Africa*. Stanford, Calif.: Stanford University Press, 1960.

Vermeil, Pierre. "Le parti démocratique gabonais." *Le Mois en Afrique,* no. 176–177 (August–September, 1980): 9–10.

Weinstein, Brian. *Eboué*. New York: Oxford University Press, 1971.

———. *Nation-Building on the Ogooué*. Cambridge, Mass.: Harvard University Press, 1966.

About the Book and Author

Formerly one of the four territories that made up French Equatorial Africa, Gabon maintains close ties with its former colonizer. Since independence in 1960, this republic has undergone political and economic turmoil—disorders often reflecting the national interests of the French and the limits of Gabonese autonomy. These upheavals have included attempts by its first president, Léon Mba, to establish a centralized one-party regime, a coup d'état led by young army officers, a highly controversial French military intervention that returned Mba to power, and the restored appearance of economic and political stability in the 1980s under President Omar Bongo.

French interests—and those of a number of other countries—are based on Gabon's extensive natural wealth. Significant deposits of petroleum, iron ore, manganese, and uranium provide a powerful incentive for external economic involvement. At the same time, fluctuations in the international market, declining petroleum production, and questionable government spending policies have prompted economic crises and internal political disturbances. A captive of its natural riches, Gabon also struggles with a lack of identity, its future dependent on forces substantially beyond its control.

In exploring the development of Gabon, Dr. Barnes also examines the nature of the country's political and economic systems and their colonial antecedents. Dependence on France and the multinational corporate restraints on national aspirations are examined in order to assess the prospects for a viable, independent state.

James F. Barnes is associate professor of political science at Ohio University.

Index

151